Stimulating Emerging Story W

Stimulating Emerging Story Writing! Inspiring children aged 3–7 offers innovative and exciting ways to inspire young children to want to create stories and develop their emerging story writing skills. This practical guide offers comprehensive and informed support for professionals to effectively engage 'child authors' in stimulating story writing activities.

Packed full of story ideas, resource suggestions and practical activities, the book explores the various ways that professionals can help young children to develop their understanding and use of the six key elements of story, these being character, setting, plot, conflict, resolution and ending. All of the ideas in the book are designed to support a setting's daily writing provision such as mark-making opportunities, role play and using simple open-ended play resources.

Separated into two parts and with reference to the EYFS and Key stage 1 curricula, this creative new text provides professionals with tried-and-tested strategies and ideas that can be used with immediate effect. Chapters include:

- Creating characters
- The plot thickens
- Inspired ideas
- Resourcing the story stimulation

This timely text is the perfect guide for inspiring young children aged 3–7 in the classroom and will be an essential resource for practitioners, teachers and students on both early years and teacher training courses.

Simon Brownhill is a Senior Teaching Associate in the Faculty of Education at the University of Cambridge, UK.

Stimulating Emerging Story Writing!

Inspiring children aged 3–7

Simon Brownhill

Contributions by Emma Hughes-Evans

LONDON AND NEW YORK

First published 2016
by Routledge
2 Park Square, Milton Park, Abingdon, Oxon OX14 4RN

and by Routledge
711 Third Avenue, New York, NY 10017

Routledge is an imprint of the Taylor & Francis Group, an informa business

British Library Cataloguing in Publication Data
A catalogue record for this book is available from the British Library

Library of Congress Cataloging in Publication Data
A catalog record has been requested

ISBN: 978-1-138-80484-5 (hbk)
ISBN: 978-1-138-80485-2 (pbk)
ISBN: 978-1-315-75267-9 (ebk)

Typeset in Sabon
by Saxon Graphics Ltd, Derby

To 'Simon's Group' – past, present and future

Contents

Acknowledgements

It is with the most heartfelt thanks that the following people are recognised:

- To Emma for all of her incredible hard work in editing each of the Ideas which made up the first 'messy' draft of this book, enriching them all with her numerous contributions – *thank you, thank you, thank you!*
- To my amazing family – Mom and Pop, Sugarfluff and Bro, Geoff and Eve, and Wilf the dog – thank you for your continued love and support.
- To the Fishers – I am very lucky to know and have you in my life.
- To all of my friends, both established, online and new – thanks for being my bud.
- To my godson, Curtis Jnr – I cannot tell you how proud I am to have been asked to be a part of your life.
- To the many wonderful colleagues I work with at the University of Cambridge, many of whom I consider to be my friend – thank you for your support.
- To all of the interpreters, co-trainers, administration, senior management and many trainers I have had the good fortune of working with on the CoE programme in Kazakhstan.
- All at Routledge, especially Annamarie and Sarah, for their diligent efforts in putting me in print once again.

Thank you all very much indeed.

SPB

Glossary and abbreviations

The following terms/abbreviations are used consistently throughout this professional book:

aka	also known as
BBC	British Broadcasting Corporation
BEd	Bachelor of Education
BFI	British Film Institute
BTEC	Business and Technology Education Council
CACHE	Council for Awards in Care, Health and Education
CD	Compact disc
Child author	Any child or young person who mark makes/writes stories
CPD	Continuing Professional Development
DfE	Department for Education
DfEE	Department for Education and Employment
DfES	Department for Education and Skills
DVD	Digital versatile disc
EYFS	Early Years Foundation Stage (3–5+ years old)
EYTS	Early Years Teacher Status
GTC	General Teaching Council for England
HLTA	Higher level teaching assistant
ICT	Information and Communication Technology
IPD	Initial Professional Development
IWB	Interactive whiteboard
KS1	Key stage 1 (5–7 years old)
Literacy	Reading and writing
LKS2	Lower Key stage 2 (7–9 years old)
Mark making	Marks made by a child author aged 3–5+ that have meaning to them
n.d.	No date of publication indicated
NBC	National Broadcasting Company (an American commercial broadcast television and radio network)
NVQ	National Vocational Qualification
OECD	Organisation for Economic Co-operation and Development
OFSTED	Office for Standards in Education, Children's Services and Skills
PDF	Portable document format

PE	Physical Education
PGCE	Postgraduate Certificate in Education
PHSCE	Personal, Health, Social and Citizenship Education
PISA	Programme for International Student Assessment
POV	Point of view
Professional	Anyone who supports child authors in their learning, be they a volunteer, training (student) or qualified (practitioner, teaching assistant, teacher)
PTA	Parent Teacher Association
R&B	Rhythm and blues
SCITT	School-Centred Initial Teacher Training
SEND	Special Educational Needs and Disabilities
SOAR	Situations, Obstacles, Actions, Results
SATS	Standard Assessment Tests
Story	An account of imaginary or real people / beings and events told to inform, educate and entertain; synonyms include *narrative*, *tale*, *yarn*, *fable*, *fiction*
Story dictation	The recorded print version of a child author's verbalised story made by a professional
TRUCE	Teachers Resisting Unhealthy Children's Entertainment
UFO	Unidentified flying object
UK	United Kingdom
UKS2	Upper Key stage 2 (9–11 years old)
VCOP	Verbs, Connectives, Openers, Punctuation
Weekend work	Synonym for *homework*
Writing	The representation of language in a textual medium through the use of a set of signs or symbols that have meaning for both the writer (child author) and the reader

Key stage bandings

The following Key stage bandings are used in this professional book to indicate particular age groups that different ideas are recommended for:

Key stage banding	Abbreviation	Alternative reference	Age group
Early Years Foundation Stage	EYFS	Early Years	3–5*
Key stage 1	KS1	Infants	5–7

* While it is recognised that the EYFS encapsulates the 0–5+ age range (0–60+ months), for the purposes of this book the EYFS refers to young children aged 3–5+ (36–60+ months).

Professionals are kindly reminded that the Key stage bandings offered in this professional book are *merely a recommendation*; readers may wish to select and use ideas offered in Key stage bandings that are different from the one they train/work in to positively respond to the needs and abilities of the child authors that they have the good fortune of working with.

Introduction

Six small cards were shuffled and carefully dealt, face down, in a row on the table.

Go on – pick one!

The man looked at the cards for a moment, reached out and selected one, turning it over in his hand. On the card was written a question: What?

The man thought for a moment and then began to type...

What is this book all about?

This book, as its title so aptly describes, is all about stimulating story writing – 'stimulating' in the sense of arousing children's interest and enthusiasm *for* story writing and 'stimulating' in the sense of ensuring that the stories children write are interesting *in content*, both for those who write them and those who read them. The notion of 'emerging', which also appears in the title of this book, is a purposeful one as it is fully recognised that young children's abilities to effectively write stimulating stories develop over time (see Featherstone, 2012; Wiltshire Council, n.d.). With this in mind, readers will note how the words 'emerging' and 'mark making/writing' are presented interchangeably throughout this book to succinctly encapsulate the full 3–7 age range and emphasise the progression from emergent writing (in the form of marks) to independent writing (the presentation of real words) which typically occurs during the formative years of a child's schooling.

This professional book focuses its attention on helping professionals to continue to 'reinvigorate' (OFSTED, 2009: 25) emerging story writing provision in their respective settings/classrooms/schools. A detailed exploration of the different development statements for *Literacy: Writing* (EYFS) and the two dimensions which make up the Programmes of Study for Writing at KS1 – 'transcription (spelling and handwriting) [and] composition (articulating ideas and structuring them in speech and writing)' (DfE, 2013: 5) – largely fall out of the remit of this book; while the importance of these cannot be underestimated, professionals are encouraged to seek other sources for support (be they professional or academic) if their interest lies more in aspects such as writing development, handwriting, phonics or grammatical terminology. What is *central* to this book, however, is the interrelatedness of the *Themes, Principles* and *Practices* of the EYFS (see Early Education, 2012: 2) and the interconnectedness of *spoken language, reading* and *writing* in KS1 (see DfE, 2013: 3) which implicitly underpin the thinking and ideas which are presented in this book.

> Readers will note that links to the *Development Matters in the Early Years Foundation Stage (EYFS)* (Early Education, 2012) and the *English Programmes of Study: Key stages 1 and 2 – National Curriculum in England* (DfE, 2013) are *implicit* in the body of this book as opposed to them being explicit in nature; a conscious decision was made to ensure that all available wordage for the writing of this book could be channelled into providing professionals with an abundance of ways to stimulate children's emerging story writing as opposed to 'tying' every idea and suggestion to statutory and non-statutory curriculum requirements.

Quite simply, this book has been written to offer those who work with children in educational contexts with a bounty of story mark making/writing ideas, practical learning and teaching strategies, academic information and thinking, research-informed guidance, *Gold star!* suggestions, and 'tried-and-tested' resources and activities to complement, energise and enrich professionals' evolving/established story writing provision and practice. It is strongly believed that committed professionals should actively seek a multitude of ways to engage young children in exciting and purposeful emerging story writing activity as part of a balanced curriculum: this is what this book aims to provide.

The man stopped typing, stretched, and looked over at the five remaining cards on the table.

Go on – pick another!

The man selected a second card – on this card was written a different question: Why?

The man's fingers approached the keyboard...

Why has this book been written?

There are numerous reasons as to why this book has been written; these are offered in bullet point form below and are merely presented in the order in which they came to mind:

- to satisfy the author's personal desire to write;
- to help and support professionals who work with children in educational contexts with regard to emerging story writing;
- to energise emerging story writing provision and practices in educational settings and schools with regard to planning, resources, learning and teaching strategies and creative story writing ideas;

- to put the 'theory-into-practice' and the 'practice-into-theory' by making readers aware of academic thinking and research to support and strengthen professional practices associated with the adult-led teaching of emerging story writing; and
- to purposefully engage young children in rich and stimulating story mark making/writing activity.

This book has been written amidst the publication of various statistics that have recently appeared in national reports and international study findings linked to 'standards' in settings/schools and the 'achievements' of children and young people. In 2013 the OECD reported that the PISA 2012 results for the UK showed 'no change in performance' in English (p. 1) when compared with the results from PISA 2006 and PISA 2009. From a national perspective, in 2012 the DfE stated that '[w]riting is the subject with the worst performance compared with reading, maths and science at Key stages 1 and 2' (p. 3). Reported statistics highlight that:

- 33 per cent of children at the end of the EYFS in 2013 failed to reach at least the expected level in writing (DfE, 2014);
- 14 per cent of children at the end of KS1 in 2014 failed to meet the expected standard in writing (OFSTED, 2014).

It is important to stress that this book makes *no* claim in being able to directly address and rapidly reduce these concerning percentages. What it does aim to do, however, is offer professionals ways to provide young children with exciting opportunities to 'mark make/writ[e stories] for enjoyment' (OFSTED, 2009: 50) and 'engage and motivate pupils through practical, creative and purposeful [writing] activities' (p. 53). By doing this it is hoped that young children will be more motivated to *want* to write and, with focused taught input and practice, they will be able to write *well*, which in turn will positively impact on formative and summative assessment results. Readers are therefore encouraged to be mindful that the success or 'impact' of this book is *not* to be measured on the number of children who achieve or exceed governmental floor targets or 'standards' in their settings/classrooms – it is more about *stimulating* young children and instilling in them a *passion* for putting pen to paper/finger to keyboard and writing emerging stories (see Cremin, 2010).

After answering his phone the man returned to the laptop.

This time why not pick *two* cards!

The man immediately chose two cards that were next to each other. On one it read: Where?; *on the other it read:* When?

Tap-tap-tap *went the keys on the man's laptop...*

Where and when can this book be used?

There are many setting and school types in which the ideas in this book can be used; a selection is offered below:

Nursery schools	Foundation Units	Infant schools	Primary schools
Nursery (Foundation One) classes and Reception (Foundation Two) classes as part of a primary school		Reception (Foundation Two) classes as part of a primary school	
After school clubs	Holiday clubs / sessional	Childminders	Full day care providers
Free schools	Academies	Faith schools	First schools
Hospital schools	Special schools	Private / independent schools	

In light of the above, it is worth acknowledging the different professionals that this book has been written to support (the *Who this book is written for*); the table below is adapted from Brownhill (2013: 5) in an effort to summarise a selection of the wide readership that this professional book aims to serve:

Those who are training or volunteering	• Practice-based qualifications e.g. BTEC, CACHE, NVQ • Initial teacher training e.g. EYTS, BEd, PGCE, SCITT, School Direct • Education-based degrees e.g. Early Childhood, Child and Youth, Education Studies • Volunteers e.g. parent / carer helpers
Those in the infancy of their career	• Recently awarded with practice-based qualifications e.g. BTEC, CACHE, NVQ • Newly qualified teachers e.g. Early Years, Primary
Those who are established in their working role	• Class teachers e.g. Early Years, Primary, SEND, supply • Practitioners / teaching assistants / learning support / mentors / HLTAs • Co-ordinators e.g. English, Literacy • Senior management members e.g. head teachers, deputy head teachers, assistant head teachers, governing body • Lecturers e.g. college (FE) and university (HE)

The professionals identified above (and others) are encouraged to use this book in a variety of different ways to support both their initial/continuing professional development (IPD/CPD) and their provision and practice in the setting/classroom/ school. A selection of possible ideas is provided in the grid overleaf:

Learning and teaching strategies can be integrated into existing adult-led provision / literacy planning (daily, weekly, medium term)	Suggested resources (writing / practical stimuli) can be collected, made or purchased for particular year groups / Key stages	Academic and professional readings from the book can be read and discussed as part of a 'professional conversation' during a team / staff meeting
Story ideas can be used to stimulate child authors' weekend work/homework/ summer work activity	Ideas and information from the book can be used to inform action research projects currently being undertaken by professionals	Ideas can be used to support coaching and mentoring activity within the setting / school; they can also be used to contribute to lesson study preparations / activity
Network clusters can discuss, adapt and review the effectiveness of suggested ideas in this book with fellow professionals	Activities, ideas and suggestions can be shared with parents and carers during Open Days or Parent / Carer Writing Workshops	Academic and professional readings can be read and used to support the writing of coursework assignments as part of one's professional studies

There are just two cards left – pick one!

The man selected one of the cards and looked at it: Who?

'Well, I've already answered that!' *thought the man. There was thus only one card left.*

'I bet it says "How?"' *thought the man. He guessed correctly.*

How is this book organised and how can it be used?

A scan of the contents pages (pp. vii–x) indicates that this book is made up of ten chapters, each one containing nine main Ideas linked to the chapter focus and a 'Story writing "pick and mix"' to close the chapter. The book is organised into two main parts. Part I is made up of Chapters 1 to 6, each one of which focuses its attention on a different story element; these are presented in the grid below:

Chapter number	1	2	3	4	5	6
Chapter title	Creating characters!	Super settings!	The plot thickens!	Colourful conflict!	Resolving the problem/s!	All's well that ends well!
Associated story element	Character	Setting	Plot	Conflict	Resolution	Ending

Part II is made up of the four remaining chapters, each one exploring different ways to stimulate emerging story writing, namely through the use of inspired ideas (Chapter 7), resources (Chapter 8) and open-ended stimuli (Chapter 9). The final chapter (Chapter 10) addresses the 'great difficulty [of actually] getting started' (Selznick, 2012: 115) by offering professionals an array of practical and effective ways to help young child authors put pen to paper/finger to keyboard and actually mark make/write emerging stories!

Each Idea initially gives a brief explanation of the main focus and then offers suggestions that can be used and adapted for child authors across different Key stages. A *Gold star!* submission is offered at the end of each Idea to further invigorate emerging story writing provision, practice and understanding; many of these ideas are not directly connected to the main Idea described but they do serve as an integral feature to stimulating emerging story writing as a whole.

Readers can engage with this book in a number of different ways:

- a *pick and mix* approach in which ideas and suggestions are randomly selected for use;
- a *cover-to-cover* approach which allows the reader to fully understand and embrace the book as a whole;
- an *element* approach which allows professionals to focus their attention on a specific story element (chapter) that they are teaching or on an area of need for their child authors; or
- a *zone-in* approach where readers use the contents pages or the index to 'shine a spotlight' on a particular strategy or idea.

All of these approaches are perfectly acceptable and readers are actively encouraged to embrace these as part of their active use of the book.

It is recognised that readers may come across strategies or ideas that they already use; this should reassure them that they are currently utilising 'good practice' as part of their emerging story writing provision in the setting/classroom. There may be ideas that readers encounter which they feel will not work with their child authors or will need some adaption or extension to make them suitable for use; this is also considered to be 'good practice' and readers are actively encouraged to not take the ideas presented in this book simply at face value. There are likely to be some ideas that readers will immediately dismiss ('I could do better than that!'). *This is also 'good practice'!* Do use your own creative ideas; after all, this book is not (and could never be) 'the answer' but merely serves as an exciting source of story writing stimuli.

It is very much hoped that this book engages not only the young children you work with to produce wonderful stories (see Shaw, 2007), but also *you* as a professional in developing and enriching your emerging story writing knowledge and practice. *So go forth...and enjoy stimulating emerging story writing!*

> **Note!**
> At the time of writing all of the *tinyurl.com* links offered in this book were active. As information on the web is regularly changed, updated or removed, it is anticipated that some links may not work for the reader. The author apologises for this, but it is hoped that readers will recognise that this is out of the author's control.
>
> (Brownhill, 2013: 28)

The man sat back in his chair. With all of the cards having been selected there was now nothing left to do but to actually write *the book that the* Introduction *had talked about!*

Tap-tap-tap...

Part I

Story elements

Chapter 1

Creating characters!

Being human!

A primary source of 'character' for young child authors is human beings. They come in a multitude of sizes and shapes, have different personalities and temperaments, wear various kinds of clothing, and move, talk and behave in exciting and strange ways. Angelou (in Brown Agins, 2006) quite aptly states that this "diversity makes for a rich tapestry". With support from professionals, child authors can easily 'unpick' this tapestry, releasing from it wonderful human characters that can be captured in their own emerging story writing!

Early Years Foundation Stage

- Encourage child authors to create simple characters based on human beings that are in their lives e.g. *Mummy, Step Daddy, Brother Sam, Baby Jessica* or *Grampy*. Suggest that they use the real actions of human beings as the basis of their emerging story e.g. 'Dad fell down the stairs!' (story dictation, Jonah, 3.6 years old), presenting an accompanying illustration which serves as a photograph that managed to capture 'the action'!
- Carver (2005) claims that 'the surest way to make your readers care about the people in [a] story is to create and portray human characters who...talk as real people talk'. Get child authors to add speech-bubble-shaped paper or sticky labels to emerging story pictures to capture short examples of different parts of speech made by their human characters e.g. proper nouns (*Auntie! Billy!*), verbs (*Sit! Listen!*) and interjections (*Oh! Boo!*).

Key stage 1

- One of the basic components that express a character's character is their appearance (Boryga, 2011). Get child authors to create a distinctive 'look' for their lead human character by looking at illustrations in picture books, clothing magazines or via safe internet image searches. Ensure that this 'look' is expressed not only in any illustrations child authors present but is also described in their written story about being unique e.g. *Fred wos scrufi. He had no hom. He wos a slip on the bentch.* ('Fred was scruffy. He had no home. He was asleep on the bench.' Nazipa, 5.8 years old, story extract.)

- Encourage child authors to 'broaden their horizons' when thinking about human beings as characters for stories about outings e.g. *wider family members, local community members, historical figures, stars of the stage and screen* or *royalty*. Create collaborative '3D character profiles' by temporarily attaching descriptive sticky labels on the body of a human profile structure (a child author). Use these profiles to inform their subsequent story writing, titles of which might include *Clever Cousins* or *The Smelly Queen*!

Gold star!

In order to survive, human beings need food and drink. Keeping well fed and hydrated is also of great benefit to their learning, depending, however, on *what* they actually consume (see Ross, 2010)! Make freely available healthy snacks and drinks in the form of fresh fruit, vegetables and water *as* child authors mark make/write so that they can *'Drink While They Think'* and *'Nibble While They Scribble'* in an effort to aid the emerging story writing process. Also use food and drink as a stimulus for child authors' mark making/writing – *what happens to human characters when they consume different foods/drinks* (think bananas and Eric Twinge aka *Bananaman*)?!

It's all in the name!

One of the first decisions that child authors need to make is not just *who* is going to be in their story but what *names* they are going to give their characters, especially the lead protagonist (Klems, 2012). Memorable stories contain memorable characters that have memorable names – think *The Gruffalo, Dora the Explorer* and *Spot (the dog)*. Professionals can support child authors to select or create names for their story character by using those that are found in baby books, telephone directories, newspapers, holy texts, film credits and street names on maps. Other inspiring suggestions are offered below!

Early Years Foundation Stage

- Encourage child authors to orally decide on character names that have personal meaning to them e.g. those associated with their family/carers and friends, examples of which include *Mummy, Pop* (Dad), *Mama* (Grandma), *Sally* (their best friend) and the names of their (step)siblings. Encourage them to mark make/write an emerging story about the day they wake up to find their house is made of chocolate or the night they cannot get to sleep.
- For non-human story characters suggest that child authors use pets' names or simple names that are easy for them to sound out e.g. *Tim, Bess* and *Meg*; an alternative is to use the common name of the animal e.g. *Duck, Cat* and *Dog*. Get them to mark make/write an emerging story on grey paper that represents fog. *Who do they literally bump into one fog-filled morning?* Alternatively, consider using green paper to represent grass. *'Who is hiding in the meadow?'*

Key stage 1

- Help child authors to appreciate how characters' names can be based on/used to reflect their personality e.g. *Mr. Happy* (Hargreaves, 2008) and *Grumpy* (Disney's *Snow White and the Seven Dwarves*). Use 'think-alouds' to explore this idea as a group/class (see Wilhelm, 2013). *How does the character's personality change in their written story when they fall in love, lose their keys or discover mice in the food cupboards?*
- Suggest that child authors embrace the practice of Stan Lee (*Marvel Comics*) by giving their story characters alliterative names – *Pamela Pumpkin; Skippy Stanton* – so that they are memorable to both the reader and child author. They could also offer a different spelling of a character's name to make them memorable e.g. *Jhon* (John), *Hanna* (Hannah) or *Alys* (Alice). Get child authors to write a story which opens with a *knock-knock-knocking* on a door. *'What happens when the door is answered? Who is behind the door? What do they want?'*

Gold star!

It is not only character names that child authors can have fun selecting or creating; this could also apply to selecting or creating their own! *A Series of Unfortunate Events* by Lemony Snicket (2006) is actually the 'pen name', 'nom de plume' or 'literary double' for Daniel Handler. Suggest that child authors might like to write under a pseudonym for emerging stories that are going to be presented on a classroom display – *can parents/carers/peers work out who actually wrote the story?*

Act your age!

A basic consideration when constructing a character for a story relates to how old the character is. Hardy (2014) suggests that in some cases 'age doesn't matter': is it really necessary to know the age of *Pingu* or *Elmer* (McKee, 2007)? It obviously helps if readers (and child authors) can relate to story characters in some way; one way of achieving this is by assuming that there is an 'age match'. However, this does not necessarily mean that story characters have to behave in the way their age would suggest – think of *Mrs Armitage and the Big Wave* (Blake, 2000)!

Early Years Foundation Stage

- *Baby:* Get child authors to close their eyes and imagine that they find a wand while playing in the back garden/local park. Encourage them to describe the great fun they have *swishing* it about until they accidently cast a magic spell over Step Mummy or Daddy who wake up the next morning and start behaving just like a baby! Get them to mark make/write an amusing emerging story about different things that they get up e.g. *crying for a bottle, wanting to be cuddled, wearing a bib* or *sucking on a dummy!*

- *Toddler:* Invite child authors to think about their younger siblings who were/are at what is commonly referred to as the 'Terrible Twos' (or 'Threenagers') stage of their development. *'What kinds of things did/do they get up to?'* (See http://tinyurl.com/nzsmgjx and http://tinyurl.com/cmbow5w for suggestions.) Use role play to bring these behaviours 'alive', encouraging child authors to mark make/write an emerging 'turbulent tale' about the noisy/messy mischief that the toddlers caused/cause e.g. *tearing all the toilet paper off the roll, throwing all of the pots and pans out of the cupboards* or *picking the heads off the flowers in the garden. 'Are they* really *being naughty?'*

Key stage 1

- *Parent/carer:* As a piece of weekend work, get child authors to follow a parent/carer around for a day, making a note/drawing pictures/taking digital images of all of the different things that they do e.g. *making breakfast, washing the car, food shopping* and *mowing the lawn.* Support child authors in using this information to either write a true 'Day-in-the-life-of...' story or a fictitious 'Grown up day' where they [the child author] have to take on the role of a parent/carer due to illness/absence/a dare!
- *Teenager:* Children seem to either want to look and act older than they really are or are being forced to grow up too quickly (see DfE, 2011). Give child authors a piece of black card which has a keyhole cut out of the middle of it. Let them look through it – *what do they 'see' themselves doing in the future as a teenager – singing in a band? Buying cool clothes? Playing sports with their friends?* Invite them to write down their ideas as part of a futuristic story about their hopes, dreams and aspirations. *'What do you want to be like/do when you are older?'*

Gold star!

Santoso (2009) describes how many great ideas are scribbled on cocktail napkins, toilet paper and the back of envelopes, letters and grocery bills due to people 'having no paper to write it down' on. Ensure that child authors are never short of a healthy supply of scrap paper, notebooks, sticky labels, 'shaped sheets', cardboard bookmarks, pads, paper writing cubes, journals and 'gem jotters' when mark making/writing emerging stories (see Mayesky, 2014, for further suggestions).

How do I look?

'Writers and readers both agree that, in fiction, one area that is of great importance is good characterisation' (Carter, 2012: 103). One way of achieving this is by making story characters visually distinctive: think *Rapunzel* and her *extremely* long blonde hair; think *Quasimodo* and his hunchback. Encourage child authors to give their story characters a distinguishing physical feature that will help to 'lock' them in the minds of the reader (and the child author) long after they have been read (and written)!

Early Years Foundation Stage

- Show child authors *YouTube* episodes of *The Mr. Men Show*, asking them to identify the individual colours of different characters. Invite them to draw their favourite *Mr. Man* or *Little Miss* character but colour them in using a *different* hue/tone/shade. Support child authors in mark making/writing an emerging story to explain why their colour is different e.g. *they have been sunbathing, they have fallen into some paint* or *they have eaten too many sweets!*
- Encourage child authors to talk about the physical size of different *Flanimals* (Gervais, 2007) in terms of their height, length and weight. Offer child authors modelling materials to create a new 3D Flanimal. Help them to mark make/write an emerging 'back story' as to why they are the physical size they are e.g. 'He's big 'cause he had loads of chips as a wee baby'. (story dictation, Molly, 4.3 yrs)

Key stage 1

- Challenge child authors to design a new hairstyle for Cupcake the clown using coloured wool that can be cut, arranged and glued onto a piece of silver card which represents a hairdresser's mirror. Build descriptive vocabularies by getting child authors to talk about the texture/style/appearance/amount/treatment/colour of the hair *as* they design (for suggestions see http://tinyurl.com/koynj4r). Weave descriptions of the hair into their short story about Cupcake's new hairdo. *'Why did Cupcake want/have to have a new hairstyle? How do the other clowns/audiences at the circus react to it when it is revealed as part of Cupcake's act?'* Read *Crazy Hair Day* (Saltzberg, 2008) as inspiration.
- Use PHSCE opportunities to get child authors thinking about how they feel about people they see who have tans, bruises, spots, dry skin, tattoos, boils, birthmarks, moles, vitiligo, scars, warts, freckles and wrinkly skin. *'How might characters in a story of transformation* (think *The Ugly Duckling*) *respond to individuals with one (or more) of these skin features? How might their views change by the end of their story and why do they change?'* Write this up as a reminder that we are *all* beautiful, no matter how we look.

Gold star!

Baldwin (2008: 64) recommends that professionals '[e]ncourage students to create unique characters with distinctive features that their readers will be able to visualize'. Broaden child authors' awareness of visually distinctive features by considering one (or more) of the following attributes to make their story characters 'stand out':

(continued)

Pets (on their shoulder – *parrot* – or under their arm – *dog*)		Glass eye	Posture (do they stand to attention or slouch?)	
Muscles	Eye-patch	Broken arm/leg – slings and casts	Big ears (think *Dumbo*)	Chicken legs (thin)
Piercings and tattoos	Hats, scarves and gloves	Beer belly	Yellowing/ white teeth	Enormous bottom(!)
Dreadlocks and bald spots	Disabled – wheelchair	Wearing pyjamas in the day	Masks	Make-up – garish/none
Bags under their eyes	Red rosy cheeks	Glasses/ shades	Jewellery – rings, necklaces	Double/treble chin

Use toys such as *Mr. Potato Head* and board games such as *Guess Who?* to support child authors' understanding and appreciation of visually distinctive character features.

Cultural enrichment!

Ask a child author to talk about one of their own made-up stories that involves characters from different cultures and they might struggle. *Is this because child authors do not see these characters as being 'different'?* Whatever the reason, there remains a limited number of published stories with black and ethnic minority characters, a finding which Laniyan-Amoako (2010) aims to address. With Temean (2010) claiming that 'a writer could add depth to a character if they...include the flav[o]ur of a different culture's background in their writing' it is only right and proper that we encourage child authors to 'bang the drum' for diversity (Blackman quoted in Ward, 2013) through their emerging story mark making/writing.

Early Years Foundation Stage

- Offer child authors play resources which reflect different cultures e.g. *cooking utensils, dressing-up clothes* and *artefacts*. Support them in mark making/writing an emerging story about their favourite item by magically personifying it e.g. 'The wok – he winked at me!' (story dictation, Geraldine, 3.5 yrs). Consider using the story *The Magic Porridge* as a source of inspiration.
- Play examples of cultural music in the setting, allowing child authors to move freely to the sounds and rhythms heard with scarves and ribbons. Draw pictures and mark make/write an emerging story about a fictional event that they feel this music would be played at e.g. *birthdays, festivals* and *celebrations* such as *New Year* and *weddings*: '*What exciting things could happen to characters during these events?*'

Key stage 1

- Provide child authors with opportunities to voluntarily try a range of culturally diverse food samples during snack time and cookery lessons. Encourage them to weave these foods into a written story about an exciting sleepover at their friend's house e.g. *having a culturally diverse midnight snack, sneaking sweets from the kitchen* or *giving a pet unwanted/disliked food under the dining table. 'What if eating this food caused strange and exciting things to happen to your body – what would these changes be and what would you then be able to do?'*
- Visit the local art gallery or display artwork (real or replicas) around the classroom that has either been created by artists from different cultures or depicts people and places from other countries. Support child authors in using this as visual stimuli for an exciting story based on one of the pieces of artwork e.g. *what amazing things take place when their story character tries on the African mask* (think the film *The Mask*) or *what happens when the tiger finally makes its 'surprise' appearance* (see http://tinyurl.com/6cgb29v)?

Gold star!

TeachUSWrite (2008) asserts that: '[W]hen it comes to teaching kids writing, one of the most important strategies to teach is how to write a hook. The hook is the very first sentence in the [story], and a good one creates a lasting impression with the reader.' Visit http://tinyurl.com/ndpr8gm to see how the eight identified types of hooks – <u>Question</u>, Quote, <u>Onomatopoeia</u>, Poem, Song, <u>Interjection</u>, *Startling Statistic* and <u>Dialogue</u> – are combined with pop culture (in the form of *SpongeBob SquarePants*) to really grab the attention of young readers! Consider using oral discussion, direct teaching, modelling and focused support to help young child authors appreciate the value of appropriate hooks (underlined) in varying the way they 'open' their emerging story in verbal and/or written form.

A little bit 'out of the ordinary'!

It is said that to stand out from the crowd one needs to be a little bit 'out of the ordinary'! If child authors are going to mark make/write interesting emerging stories it is important that they think carefully about their lead character, considering ways in which they can make them appealing and intriguing by giving them unusual features and traits. This can be achieved by not only 'observing human nature' (Garber, 2002: 22), be it fictional or real, but also by imitating it!

Early Years Foundation Stage

- *Movement:* Invite child authors to experiment with different ways of moving their bodies (gross motor) in the outdoor play area, linking these movements to characters that they know or could be introduced to e.g. running (*Billy Whizz*), hopping (*Skippy* the kangaroo), tip-toe movements (*Angelina Ballerina*) and flapping (*Dumbo*). Encourage child authors to mark make/write an emerging 'story scrap' (a *very* short story) about what they or their story character are moving *away from* or *to* – think *a wasp, a bully, a ghost, Mummy, the toy shop* or *a shiny coin.*

- *Hair:* Offer child authors dolls, mannequin heads or different art resources e.g. *wool, string, twine, cotton* and *thread* to experiment with different representations of hair styles – think *frizzy, wild, slick, Afro, spikey, mullet* and *beehive.* Support child authors in mark making/writing an emerging story about a funny way their story character's hair style gets altered during the day e.g. *by the wind and rain, wearing a flat hat, using hairspray, nervously playing with it, the excessive use of hair accessories such as bows or clips* or *a bird sits on it!*

Key stage 1

- *Facial expressions:* Provide child authors with a small flat mirror for them to experiment with different facial expressions in response to verbal/written/'visual' adjectives (see http://tinyurl.com/ls7mttu). Encourage them to use these describing words to convey characters' facial expressions in response to a key event in their story set in a familiar place e.g. *surprise* when a seasonal present is opened at home or *frustration* when the results of the spelling test are given out at school.
- *Clothing:* Offer child authors clothing magazines, catalogues or dressing-up clothes which they can select from and use to assemble an outfit for their story character to wear. Get them to orally justify their choices by matching the outfit to aspects of their character's personality e.g. *bright colours for a cheery disposition* or *smart clothing for a posh person.* Support child authors in describing these outfits as part of a 'costume change' story (think *Mr Benn* – see http://tinyurl.com/q47wcx5).

Gold star!

A team of scientists, mathematicians and creative writing gurus from around the world were asked a question: '"What's the easiest way for a writer to get to know their characters?" Hands down, they all agreed the single best way is to fill out a *Character Questionnaire* for all your characters' (p. 7). Visit http://tinyurl.com/kfdmkjp, using and adapting the Character Questionnaire (pp. 8–10) as a series of prompts (be they oral or written) to help young child authors think about their characters before committing them and their adventures to paper. Introduce this idea by modelling it to child authors as part of a group carpet activity, getting older child authors to work together to initially complete an age-appropriate questionnaire (oral/written) for a well-known character, and using role play or hot-seating techniques to stimulate subsequent thinking.

Animal-tastic!

There is an abundance of children's stories with animals as central characters; this is clearly evident when one thinks of traditional tales (*The Three Little Pigs*), Aesop's fables (foxes and tortoises) or beloved children's stories (*The Very Hungry Caterpillar*; *The Gruffalo*). With most young children being 'curious about and fond of animals' (Burke and Copenhaver, 2004: 206), professionals are well placed to help child authors to choose interesting animals that serve as lead characters for their emerging written stories!

Early Years Foundation Stage

- Encourage child authors to mark make/write emerging stories about animal characters that they are familiar with e.g. *their own pets, animals they see on TV* (Peppa Pig; Timmy the sheep) or *animals found in their favourite picture books in the setting/at home.* Stimulate emerging story writing by thinking about what happens to animal characters on the day it snows multicoloured snowflakes or when they meet a magical unicorn.
- Get child authors to play with animal-based stimuli in the setting e.g. *small world animals, animal masks/picture cards/costumes/stencils* or *animal shaped sand moulds.* Use these as the basis for some emerging story writing, mark making/ writing about a chosen character's birthday party or a visit to the animal circus (see *Animal Auditions*, Hughes, 2015).

Key stage 1

- Teach child authors during their science work about different groups of animals e.g. *mammals, birds, amphibians, fishes* and *reptiles.* Encourage child authors to choose an animal from one of these different groups to diversify their lead protagonist. Get them to think, story wise, about what happens when an unwelcome visitor comes to stay with them or they decide to do some 'armchair travelling' (a virtual 'trip' that can be taken from the comfort of a chair). '*Where do you go? What do you see?*' Alternatively, they could write about a staycation.
- Use school trips to the local farm, woods, nature park or the zoo as an opportunity to develop child authors' awareness of interesting animals for one of their short stories e.g. *horses, squirrels, woodpeckers* and *elephants.* '*What happens when these animals decide to escape from their habitat (think the film* Madagascar*), have a 'duvet day', or collaboratively invent a machine that makes singing umbrellas?*'

Gold star!

Consider encouraging child authors in mark making/writing interesting emerging stories about animal characters who emulate different characteristics that they are not typically associated with:

(continued)

The 'typically characterised' animal character	The 'newly characterised' animal character	Thoughts and questions
The *proud* lion	The *shy* lion	An interesting story title perhaps?
The *shy* koala	The *snappy* koala	Are we talking about a moody marsupial or one who likes taking pictures with a digital camera?
The *snappy* crocodile	The *proud* crocodile	Proud of what – *his teeth? His kids? His tail?*

This can provide child authors with rich opportunities to develop an awareness of and work creatively with adjectives and alliteration in their mark making/writing. Visit http://tinyurl.com/km8cjtx for 'a very popular game' to play to help child authors generate and revise their knowledge and understanding of simple nouns and adjectives.

Fantastical creatures!

Lopez (n.d.) suggests that people in the Middle Ages believed that 'evil spirits, demons and beasts were real and ever present'. Fast-forward some 600+ years and the likes of Rowling (2001), Lopresti (2008) and Allan (2008) continue to delight children and adults with descriptions and images that are the stuff of myths, legends and even reality (think dinosaurs)! Through the use of appropriate visual stimuli (*pictures, posters, cartoons* and *film extracts*) professionals can support child authors in developing a desire to mark make/write emerging stories involving invented dragons, fairies, Cyclopes and mermaids!

Early Years Foundation Stage

- Offer child authors some play dough and the *fantasy play dough mats* available from http://tinyurl.com/lmqmjum. Suggest that they creatively enrich how their animal looks by adding certain features e.g. *an extra tail, a longer nose* or *a spiky bottom*! 'How do other creatures react when they see the "new and improved" animal?' (think *Elmer*). Invite them to mark make/write an emerging story where there is shock, surprise, laughter or teasing. 'How does this make the fantastical creature feel?'
- Offer child authors a selection of fantastical creature colouring sheets (see http://tinyurl.com/7s5r5vb). Using snips and scissors, invite them to 'build' a nice new fantastical creature by cutting out body parts from different creatures, piecing them together like a jigsaw. Encourage child authors to mark make/write an emerging story about their character's exploratory search for a place to sleep or their food tasting session to find out what they like to eat e.g. *little children – yum yum!*

Key stage 1

- Teach child authors the song *Puff the Magic Dragon* (see http://tinyurl.com/lk533jf). Get them to talk about how they could entice Puff out of his cave – *offer him food? Ask for his help to rescue the Princess from the evil Jester? Introduce him to a new friend* (hint hint!)? Invite child authors to 'Design a Dragon' to be Puff's new playmate. '*What adventures do they get up to together? What if the new dragon was female – could she become Puff's girlfriend or wife?*' Encourage child authors to write up one of their ideas as a short engaging story.
- Arrange a visit to the local woods where child authors can make a funky fantastical beast out of mud (see http://tinyurl.com/lh9mlog)! Encourage them to take digital images of their creations. When back in the classroom upload these images into a child-friendly word processor page, under which child authors can write (type) a short comical story about their fantastical creature and their love/hatred of being dirty/clean!

Gold star!

Think of a die/dice and professionals automatically think of mathematics! *Not so!* Dice can be used as an engaging resource to stimulate child authors' storytelling/emerging story writing. Professionals are encouraged to visit the following websites to aid and assist their storytelling/mark making/writing 'dice provision' in their setting/classroom/school:

EYFS	KS1
• http://tinyurl.com/mpskl4a • http://tinyurl.com/ps9sumx	• http://tinyurl.com/p3dybvw • http://tinyurl.com/n5s9e3s

The generation-name!

Unfortunately there is no magic formula for helping child authors come up with the perfect story character name, although excessively long character names should be avoided – see *The Boy With The Long Name* (http://tinyurl.com/kkv39mn)! Effective professionals can support child authors by using a range of effective practical strategies such as wordplay, association and rhyme to assist them in generating names for their story characters as the ideas below suggest!

Early Years Foundation Stage

- Invite child authors to select an alphabet letter from a bag of magnetic letters, an alphabet card from a set of face-down/fanned-out alphabet cards or a letter from a chalked-out alphabet hopscotch in the outdoor play area. Consider using their developing phonic knowledge to generate characters' names which start with the letter they chose e.g. *R for Ruben* or *L for Lucy*. Develop child authors' alphabet knowledge by using both lower- and uppercase letters depending on their age and ability. Support child authors in mark making/writing an emerging story solely about 'the chosen one' e.g. *Oscar's bath* or *Mia's chair*.

- Encourage child authors to name animal characters using onomatopoeic words e.g. *Fizz, Tick-Tock* and *Beep*. Generate these names by going on exploratory sound walks, playing sounds CDs or singing *Old MacDonald* where there are new animals on the farm such as frogs (*Ribbit ribbit!*), owls (*Hoot hoot!*) and chinchillas (*Squeak!*). Use these sounds as the basis of a 'What-Is-Making-That-Noise?' emerging story in which story characters go in 'search for the sound'! Consider adding flaps to story illustrations to enhance 'the search' element of the tale (see http://tinyurl.com/ookx3fo for inspiration).

Key stage 1

- Provide child authors with a range of picture books and invite them to make a written list of any story characters' *names* that they like, *not* the actual character (although this is likely to influence whether they like the character's name or not!). Suggest that they 'play' with these names by changing just one letter to create a new one e.g. *Sunny* becomes *<u>H</u>unny*; *Pippa* becomes *P<u>e</u>ppa*! Encourage them to mark make/write an emerging story which helps to explain how their story character got their name e.g. *they like* Honey Nut Loops (the cereal) or *they spend their days nibbling on peppers* (they are a rabbit!). '*What happens when these foods 'run out'?*'
- Get child authors to write individual names (personal and family/surname) on separate pieces of paper/card. Mix up the names and then select two to create a new name. Alternatively, cut each name in half and then put two different halves together to create a new name e.g.

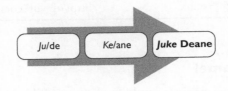

Invite child authors to write a short 'secretive' story about their character that is known by one name during the day and a different one at night. '*What are they called? What do they do at night? What do they become?*'

Gold star!

If child authors initially 'draw a blank' in naming their character suggest they get on with the actual mark making/writing of their emerging story by leaving a gap in the text (if writing by hand) or inserting a line/alphabet letter/series of spaces (if typing using ICT applications) to indicate where the character's name is needed; this can be inserted later on. They may eventually decide to name their character with a *single* letter, particularly when one thinks of the characters Q and M (*James Bond*), Mr. T (*The A Team*) and Malcolm X.

Story writing 'pick and mix' I

It is personally believed that professionals can *never* have enough learning and teaching strategies and practical ideas for the emerging story writing classroom. To keep emerging story writing fresh and interesting for child authors it is important to engage them with new and exciting ideas to stimulate both the mark making/writing process and product. Virtually all of the ideas in this collection are not attributed to a particular age phase but is offered more as a 'pick and mix' of suggestions for professionals to select from and adapt in response to the mark making/writing needs of their learners – *put an 'X' by any that you think you might try out!*

X

	Trump story: Encourage child authors to write a short story about a couple of friends who try to outdo each other at a party (various types) with the gifts they buy for the special boy/girl. Have them end the story with the friends understanding that no matter how big or expensive the gift their friendship is more appreciated.
	Smelly story characters: Enrich child authors' characterisation by inviting them to give their lead characters a 'scented presence' in their emerging story – this could relate to the *perfume or aftershave* that they wear, their *body odour* (ugh!), or it could indicate where they have been e.g. *a farm, a chocolate factory* or *a scented garden for the blind. 'How do others react to the smell? What if their smell was stolen – think* The Stolen Smell (Hamilton and Weiss, 2007) *– how would they get it back?'*
	Story title: Offer child authors the story title *The Pillow of Dreams.* Support them in developing an emerging story by suggesting that story characters who lay their head on the pillow at night experience the most *spectaculant* (a mixture of 'spectacular' and 'brilliant') dreams. *'What will their dream be about tonight?'* Offer child authors pillows to rest on as they mark make/write.
	Story size: A key aspect of child authors' mark making/handwriting is the size of the marks/symbols that they form – young children typically produce large marks/large letters which get smaller as they progress through the different stages of the handwriting developmental model (see Hill, 2006). Offer child authors opportunities for *giants, superheroes, plane passengers* and *birds in the sky* to read their emerging stories by presenting them on the outdoor/playground area in big chalked letters!
	Story balls: Facilitate a frenzy of emerging story writing by getting child authors to individually draw/mark make/write a word or sentence on a piece of paper which is 'balled up' and thrown across the carpet/table to another child author who has to add a new drawing/mark/word/sentence to continue the truly 'emerging' story. Review the stories generated, considering ways to improve them through the process of rewriting (apt for upper KS1).
	Story flap book: Visit http://tinyurl.com/nohanqj, supporting child authors in retelling a simple fairytale or fable by making a flap book (refer to the instructions on p. 1 of the PDF). Adapt the flap book template for younger child authors by reducing the number of flaps and removing the labels on the front of each flap. Support young child authors by using digital images, stamps, stencils, 'lick and stick' images, stickers, key letters, words and short phrases so that they can quickly recall the different sections which make up the known story.

Chapter 2

Super settings!

Welcome to my home!

The DfES (2001: 5) state that '[b]asing stories in a well-known place is a technique used by many authors'. It is personally believed that there is no story setting more familiar to child authors than 'the home'. The beauty of this as a backdrop for a story means that they do not necessarily have to create the setting seeing as for most of them it already exists! With support from professionals and a little creativity, child authors can use the home as a rich 'base' for some stimulating emerging story writing!

Early Years Foundation Stage

- Encourage child authors to use play-based opportunities (small world/role play areas) to explore different rooms found in the home e.g. *the kitchen/bedroom/living room*. Invite them to mark make/write an emerging story about something secret which takes place in their favourite room (be it real or play-based) e.g. *drinking juice under a blanket in the living room* or *making a surprise alien birthday cake for Daddy in the kitchen*.
- Read *The Tiger Who Came to Tea* (Kerr, 2006). Suggest that child authors mark make/write about an alternative animal that comes to their home for breakfast, dinner/supper or a snack, offering visual stimuli (think *toys/non-fiction books/web-based images*) to support their animal selection. *'What happens when the animal comes into your home – do they ransack the bathroom, fall asleep in front of the fire or gobble up Granny?'*

Key stage 1

- As a piece of weekend work, suggest that child authors go on a treasure hunt at home. Invite them to take digital images or create a visual display of some of the items they found at school. Support them in writing a short 'finders, keepers' story about what was found and where e.g. *I fawd a red ring undr Mummys bed. Its myn now.* (Fiona, 5.4 yrs.)
- Teach child authors the music hall song *When Father Papered the Parlour* (see http://tinyurl.com/qh5qn3o). Encourage them to imagine a home improvement disaster at their home e.g. *holes in floors*, *leaking pipes* or *falling ceilings*. Support them in adding some interesting detail to their disaster story by modelling how to

make the setting suitably hazardous e.g. *Live wires hung from the ceiling. The baby tried to swing like Tarzan on them!*

Gold star!

With ICT playing an ever important role in our day-to-day lives, it is inevitable that story mark making/writing can be supported/enhanced with technological software and resources. Provide child authors with access to age-appropriate *story writing apps* (either online- or tablet-based) to aid the emerging story writing process; personal recommendations for professional exploration are offered below, all of which can be found via a *Google* web search:

StoryBook Maker	Story Patch	Toontastic	Story Ideas*	Rory's Story Cubes

* Created by Pie Corbett.

Food venues!

Anderson (2005: 5) succinctly states that 'everyone eats'. With food playing a central role in our lives, child authors should be encouraged to capitalise on this as a 'plentiful plate of possibility' for their emerging story mark making/writing. Not only can they set their stories in a variety of food *venues* (the central focus of this Idea) but they can also think about the interesting foods that are *served* there and the *significance* of them to the story, while creating a wealth of story characters with different *attitudes* and *responses* to foods that are consumed e.g. *'Mmm!'* and *'Yuck!'*

Early Years Foundation Stage

- *Home:* Offer child authors the toy tea set, encouraging them to set it up and role play having tea at home. KNOCK KNOCK! *'There's someone at the back door – whoever could that be?'* Get child authors to mark make/write an emerging story about who appears at their door – *Olaf from* Frozen? *A horse? A talking tractor?* Think about what child authors have to provide for their guest to cater for their select tastes – *snow? Carrots? Oil?*
- *Family restaurant:* Support child authors in talking about different foods that they eat at different times of the day. Invite them to mark make/write an amusing emerging story about their visit to the new *Random (Pop up) Restaurant* where they can eat breakfast at supper time or lunch at breakfast time if they want to! *What will they decide to eat and when?* Get them to draw their chosen food on a paper plate, offering their story marks/writing around the edge of the plate.

Key stage I

- *Café:* Use paired talk to get child authors thinking about times they have been with family members to the local café. *'What did you eat/drink? Who did you see there?'* Challenge them to write a story about an imaginary visit where strange things occur e.g. *the menu text keeps changing, the sponge cakes blow raspberries at customers* or *the sugar refuses to pour!* Get child authors to consider who is behind this – *a fairy? A wizard? A witch? 'Why are they doing this?'*

- *Fast food establishment:* Invite child authors to write a celebratory story about a birthday party set in a fast food restaurant – think *McDonalds* or *KFC*. In small groups explore 'problem possibilities' e.g. *the clown makes everyone cry, the food served is stone cold* or *someone gets locked in the toilet!* Ensure that child authors develop satisfactory resolutions to these different difficulties, emphasising the *healthy* food they all have as part of the celebrations.

Gold star!

Chapter 4 of McCarthy's (1998) professional book *Narrative Writing* offers a wealth of interesting ideas to enrich professional practices when supporting child authors and their emerging story mark making/writing. Visit http://tinyurl. com/n5a2xeg, paying particular attention to pp. 41–52; ideas that are personally rated include the *Grab Bag* (p. 46, apt for EYFS) and the *plot-steps* (p. 42, apt for KS1).

Shops galore!

The Open University (2014) suggests that '[c]reative writing courses and manuals often offer the advice "write what you know"'. A setting that will be known to virtually all child authors is 'the shops'. From frequent visits to the local newsagents to weekly excursions to the supermarket, child authors should be able to tap into a wealth of lived experiences to draw on in their story mark making/writing. With so many types of shops offering so many different goods and services, it is surprising that not more shop stories have been written! *Let's get child authors to change that now, shall we?!*

Early Years Foundation Stage

- Support child authors in setting up and playing in a *florist* role play area (see http://tinyurl.com/nhr7l3c). When the shop is 'closed' at the end of the session, get them to think about what the flowers do at night – *sing? Dance? Play in the sandpit?* Encourage child authors to mark make/write an emerging story about one of these nocturnal activities. *'What evidence is there of this activity actually happening? For example, is the Sing-Along CD in the CD player? Are there petals in the sand?'*
- Read *The Shopping Basket* (Burningham, 2000). Get child authors to imagine what they would put in their shopping basket if Mummy asked them to get food for tea from the *supermarket*. *'Who might try to take things out of your basket on the way home?'* Invite child authors to draw groceries inside a basket-shaped piece of paper, mark making/writing an emerging story underneath about different 'bullies' e.g. 'Daddy took the chocolate' (story dictation, Sally, 4.1 yrs).

Key stage 1

- Organise an educational visit to the local shopping area where child authors can learn about different types of shops e.g. *fish and chip*, *newsagents*, *chemists* and *opticians*. Challenge child authors to use one of these as the setting for a comical caper e.g. *the day the shop owner slipped into the deep fat fryer, Granny falling asleep on the magazine rack* or *a mix up with the prescriptions resulting in someone growing another nose!*
- Show child authors web-based images of *hairdressing salons* and *barber shops*. Invite them to write a 'disaster' story where a story character gets their hair cut and it is not in the style that they hoped! Support illustrations with vivid written descriptions by referring to the cut, colour and sensory qualities of the hair – visit http://tinyurl.com/np6kpdm for suggestions, 'visualising' adjectives with wool, string, plastercine or fake hair. *'How did the hairdresser/barber try to repair the damage?'*

Gold star!

Grossman (2013) energetically discusses the notion of 'Snapchat Stories' which gives online social media 'users the option to string together pictures and videos taken throughout the day'. As child authors should not register for the likes of *Facebook* and *Twitter* until they are 13 years of age, encourage them to 'string together' their written efforts using photographs (EYFS) and digital scans/photocopies (KS1) of their written stories. Alternatively, get children from KS2 (LKS2 and UKS2) to read their snappy (short, exciting) stories to younger children in the school; they thus serve as the visiting 'Snapchat' author to the class!

Sporty locations!

Children are born to move and so sports, or pursuits which involve them being physically active, are important for their development and their health in later life. With many young male readers favouring stories that are set within a sporting context – see *Winners Never Quit!* (Hamm, 2006) – sporty locations offer the perfect backdrop to effectively engage both male *and* female child authors to *want* to mark make/write a stimulating emerging story!

Early Years Foundation Stage

- *Outdoor play area:* Get child authors to mark make/write an emerging story about something exciting that has happened to them in the setting's outdoor play area e.g. *playing kiss-chase with their 'boy-'/'girlfriend', bumping trikes into one another by accident* or *batting a sponge ball onto someone's head* (**BOINK!**)*!*
- *Back garden:* Encourage child authors to talk about competitive games that they play with siblings or friends in their back garden or at the local park e.g. *climbing the ladder the quickest to get to the tree house, running around the edge of the*

garden in the shortest time or *pedalling go-karts as fast as possible along the footpath*. Inquire as to whether they would like to contribute an emerging story about one of these games for a class anthology about competition.

Key stage 1

- *Playground:* Show child authors a picture (web-based) of bored children. *'Why are they bored? Is their playground at school not exciting* [hint hint!]*?'* Invite them to write a short story about a school with a bland playground. *'What do the teachers and children decide to do to it "jazz it up"?'* Allow child authors to work on their story 'in situ' with writing clipboards and pencils.
- *Local park/field:* Take child authors to the local park/field. Get them to use their different senses to explore the location, generating a list of 'concrete' adjectives to describe the setting. Show them how to weave these into an exciting story about sporty activities which they/their characters engage in there e.g. *chasing after a Frisbee, playing on the park play area* or *flying a colourful kite*.

Gold star!

Help child authors by using the Olympics or sporting/activity events that take place at the setting/school as a source of reference to 'inform the action' in child authors' emerging sporty story writing – think *sports days, outdoor play periods, PE lessons, after-school sports clubs, Walk to School weeks, Activ8* or *Wake and Shake*. Encourage older child authors to then choose a particular sporting star (real or cartoon-based) as a character in their emerging story. *'What happens the day David Beckham comes round for a "kick about" or Tom Daly visits for a bit of a splash?'*

Where the 'other half' live!

Altman (2010: 1) asserts that '[o]n a very basic, biological basis, scientists say we humans are hardwired to be fascinated with celebrity'. Indeed, our love of celebrity magazines, reality TV and celebrity game shows – think *Through the Keyhole* – help to satisfy our desire to see where and how 'the other half' live. The homes of the rich and famous (or well-known) can serve as stimulating settings for child authors' emerging stories as they offer rich possibilities in relation to the *where* (place) element of setting, as highlighted in the suggestions below.

Early Years Foundation Stage

- Get child authors to find images in picture books of the homes of well-known story characters e.g. *Dora the Explorer, Bob the Builder* or *The Three Little Pigs*. Get them to draw/paint the house they would most like to visit, mark making/writing an emerging creative story about what they would like to do there e.g. 'I want to play ball with Bob' (story dictation, Sanjeet, 3.4 yrs).

- Encourage child authors to pretend they are Jack (from *Jack and the Beanstalk*, or *Jackie* for the girls) or comic characters such as *Richie Rich* or *Mayda Munny*, offering them paper play money and plastic coins that represent part of their wealth. '*What expensive things would you buy with it to make your bedroom/house look really posh or beautiful?*' Invite them to mark make/write about their extravagant purchases as part of an emerging story with reference to catalogues e.g. *big beds, massive teddies, gigantic rugs* or *a swimming pool for their fish!*

Key stage 1

- Offer child authors magazine cuttings about the homes of rich people (real/fictional) e.g. *The Queen (a palace)*, *Barbie (a Dream House)* or *One Direction (an upmarket apartment)*. Invite them to set a scavenger hunt story (see http://tinyurl.com/6eexwbk) in one of these houses, using the cuttings as a reference point to help them accurately describe different rooms in terms of their colour, size and shape. '*What exciting things do you find there?*'
- If there is an impressive house or building in the locality take child authors to visit it. Engage their different senses to stimulate what Peat (2002: 56) refers to as 'location writing' (see http://tinyurl.com/mdbnnu8 for more information). '*What can you smell/hear?*' Use this information to enrich setting descriptions in their exciting 'Day-with-a-Star' story. '*What do you get up to together?*' If it is not possible to undertake a visit or if the place is not local e.g. it is in other country, consider using photographs or web-based images.

Gold star!

Efforts to use ICT to support/enhance the learning and teaching experiences of child authors are important to maintain their willing engagement with emerging story mark making/writing activity. Visit http://tinyurl.com/3xhq66b or http://tinyurl.com/lwfo5yc for a wealth of literacy resources which can be adapted and used by professionals on the IWB or by child authors on individual/shared computers, laptops and tablets. Consider how these resources can stimulate children's storytelling (see Miller and Pennycuff, 2008) which can in turn inform their emerging story writing.

Various vehicles!

Newcombe (2013) claims that that '[v]ehicles and transport are often the centre of great interest from young children'. Indeed, cars, diggers, boats and planes serve as staple toys for children to play with, particularly boys. Support from professionals can help child authors to locate 'the action' in their emerging story via a wealth of setting possibilities depending on the vehicle(s) that they choose and where their story characters decide to go in them!

Early Years Foundation Stage

- Offer child authors a range of toy vehicles to play with in the water tray or sand pit. Invite them to mark make/write an emerging story about a seaside adventure involving selected vehicles e.g. *exploring the deep blue sea with the* Rainbow Fish *in an underwater submarine* or *digging in the sand to find the Golden Shell.* Help child authors to add real water marks or sand to their drawings with a paint brush/glue to enhance their illustrations of the 'sensory' setting that their story takes place in.
- Offer child authors a ride on a 'magic carpet' (rolled out mat on the floor). Model how to verbally describe different locations that they 'fly over' e.g. *'Look! I can see lots and lots of tall trees and rich green leaves – we're flying over the jungle!'* Offer child authors magic-carpet-shaped paper on which they can mark make/write an emerging story about a new and exciting place that they could visit e.g. *Burger World* or *China!* Think *Aladdin* for inspiration.

Key stage 1

- Show child authors web-based images of recreational vehicles that story characters can holiday in e.g. *tent trailers, caravans, campervans, pop-up caravans, motor homes* and *camper trailers.* Get them to imagine they have woken up after a long journey and have arrived at their holiday destination. *Where are they? 'Remember: don't just tell us – paint a picture with words for us!'* Encourage them to describe what they can see and hear – *can readers (peers) work out where they are from their descriptive written clues?*
- Invite child authors to co-write a new *Thomas the Tank Engine* story with Christopher Awdry, creating a new character in the form of a steam engine, a narrow gauge engine, rolling stock or a non-rail vehicle (see http://tinyurl.com/f74uo – 8.2 *Thomas the Tank Engine and Friends*). Support child authors in describing the rolling scenery as Thomas *et al.* race to either save the railway track in the 'old part of town' or go on a trip to India to see the Hindu festival of Holi.

Gold star!

The National Literacy Trust (n.d.a) describes a *story box* as 'a miniature setting, a shoe box-sized stage with a background and objects within it relating either to a specific book, or to a common story scenario'. Support child authors in making one based on the setting of the 'current chronicle' that they are mark making/writing (see http://tinyurl.com/ow7odqw for support). Alternatively, see http://tinyurl.com/oy3qkme, http://tinyurl.com/mgoovz7 and http://tinyurl.com/kand4og (pp. 61–65) for additional information, ideas and strategies on using story boxes.

Places of interest!

Appelcline (n.d.) suggests that: '[I]n previous eras of literature, long descriptions of setting were often admired and respected, but most modern audiences want their stories to get to the action.' While young child authors are unlikely to labour their thoughts about the location of their story, it is important that they do not simply ignore their story setting but think carefully about the potential it has to fuel a good emerging story. Story potential can be found in places of interest or tourist attractions, be they local, national or international – if story characters want to visit them it is (almost) certain that *something* will happen to them there!

Early Years Foundation Stage

• Offer child authors a selection of photographs/images of places of interest in their local area e.g. *the woods, a statue/monument, the church* or *a museum*. Get them to select one of these, identifying a popular children's character (TV/book) that they meet there e.g. *Bagpuss, Ben 10, Snoopy* or *Winnie the Pooh*. Encourage them to mark make/write an emerging story about their chance encounter with their fictitious celebrity!
• Use small world play resources to raise child authors' awareness of different types of parks e.g. *theme, safari, water* and *nature*. Get them to mark make/write an emerging story about 'the jolly time' they have in one of these parks – '*What do you get up to there?*', ending the tale with something amusing e.g. *everyone gets wet on the ride* or *the lion follows the family home!*

Key stage 1

• Use non-fiction books to introduce child authors to different types of festivals e.g. *music, film, art* and *faith-related*. Get them to imagine that they are taking part in a hot-air balloon festival. '*What does your hot-air balloon look like? Who is in the hot-air balloon with you? How do you make sure you win the "night glow" race?*' Consider pasting their completed written story onto an inflated balloon and releasing it into the sky.
• Read *At the Beach* (Harvey, 2004). Get child authors to work together as a 'writing team' to generate story ideas linked to a visit to the beach with their family or friends by the sea. Encourage them to introduce an element of danger into their written story to add excitement and suspense for the reader – think *enormous waves, hungry sharks* or *whipping sandstorms*. '*How are story characters rescued from these different threats?*'

Gold star!

It is believed that a popular British playwright kept their manuscripts in the fridge to save them from potential flooding, fire or getting stolen! Invite child authors to find novel places to store their 'work in progress' or 'final drafts' both in the setting/classroom and at home e.g. in *shirt boxes, in between the pages of magazines/programmes, in time capsules, in empty plastic book covers, underneath pillow cases on their bed or rolled up inside old shoes!* Alternatively, consider using online storage systems for photographs or digital scans of child authors mark making/writing efforts e.g. *Dropbox* and *iCloud*.

International destinations!

Silvey (1995: 449) argues that: '[D]uring the first half of the twentieth century, publishers of children's books made an effort to provide stories about foreign lands.' As such, children now have access to a growing wealth of stories set in countries right across the globe – think *Handa's Surprise* (Browne, 2006). By tapping into, for example, the culture, sights, languages, history, cuisine and music of different countries, child authors can use this to enrich their 'international fiction' (Garrett, 1996) that is set in international destinations.

Early Years Foundation Stage

- When it is Chinese New Year provide child authors with access to engaging activities that help them to celebrate it e.g. *making Chinese dragons, lanterns, masks* and *celebration cards* (see http://tinyurl.com/outdhrq). Get child authors to mark make/write an emerging story about their search for the New Year dragon using their lantern or a ride that they take on its back. *'Where is the dragon hiding?/Where do you go with the dragon?'*
- Read *The Beautiful Butterfly* (Sierra, 2000). Offer child authors sugar paper and snips/scissors for them to cut out a butterfly shape. Support them in mark making/writing an emerging story on its wings about a day out that the butterfly and her husband have in Spain with them and the 'underwear' King. *'Where do you go? What do you see? Where do you play? What makes you laugh during the day?'*

Key stage 1

- Read aloud one of the ten story books listed at http://tinyurl.com/3op88un to introduce child authors to the Arctic region. Get them to imagine that one chilly morning at home they wake up and find an Inuit/penguin stood at the foot of their bed carrying a bag of ice cubes! *'What is his/her name? How did he/she end up there? What are the ice cubes for? How do you get the Inuit/penguin home before their ice cubes melt?'* Consider presenting the written story on a paper ice cube (die template – see http://tinyurl.com/k9nos42).
- Show child authors pictures of the Australian Outback, emphasising the vastness of the landscape and the extraordinary heat! Talk to child authors about a magic camera which transports users to the place in the picture that they have taken a digital image of. *'Who do you meet there?'* (See http://tinyurl.com/ycbbfua for ideas.) *'What do you do together? How do you survive in this harsh environment? Remember: don't forget the camera!'*

Gold star!

Vertsman (2014) offers a wonderful list of children's story books that are set in different countries around the world. Ensure that examples of these are freely made available for child authors, along with non-fiction texts, so that they can be used as a constant reference point when trying to capture select elements of the country in their story mark making/writing/illustrations e.g. *colours, clothing, smells, dialect, architecture, aspects of faith* and *artefacts*.

The sea and the sky (space)!

Professionals will have little difficulty in being able to name the famous story character who claimed that the sky was falling!* There are many children's stories that have been set in both the sea and the sky (space):

Key stage	Stories set in the sea	Stories set in the sky (space)
EYFS	Who's hiding under the sea?	Whatever next!
KS1	The snail and the whale	The Man on the Moon

With the support of professionals child authors can use the vastness that is the body of salt water that *covers* the Earth and the region found *above* the Earth as stimulating backgrounds for their emerging stories!

Early Years Foundation Stage

- Encourage child authors to play in the water tray with small world characters and *under the sea* resources e.g. *fish, nets, rocks* and *seaweed*. Take digital images of their play, printing these onto paper. Get child authors to mark make/write an emerging story under these images to describe the game that their small world characters were playing at the time the image was taken e.g. *the fish were playing hide and seek* or *they were playing chase with one another*.
- Offer child authors large pieces of white fabric or big balls of cotton wool to handle/play with. Get them to imagine that these are clouds in the sky. '*Who do you think lives on them? What do these characters look like? What do they do on them?*' Encourage child authors to mark make/write their emerging story on cloud-shaped pieces of white paper e.g. *Jimmy zzzzz* ('Jimmy sleeps', Jimmy, 4.4 yrs, independent writing).

---

* The answer is *Chicken Little*, otherwise known as *Henny Penny* or *Chicken Lickin*.

Key stage 1

- Invite child authors to handle a large shell (real). Challenge them to invent a new sea creature that lives inside it. *'What is it called? What does it look like? Is it a friendly creature or not?'* Suggest them to write a short story about a *well-known* sea character from the Pixar film *Finding Nemo* (e.g. 'Dory', 'Bruce' or 'Crush') who comes to visit *their* new creature. *'What do they get up to inside/outside of the shell?'*

- Show child authors simple non-fiction books and online video footage of the different planets found in space. Get child authors to select one, writing a colourful story about a character who dreams of visiting the planet and wakes up the next day actually on it! *'What happens to them when they are on the planet? How does the planet affect what they do there? How do they get home? Is it all just a dream?'*

Gold star!

'Enhance the visual' of child authors' own illustrations by providing them with liquid/gel pens and coloured paper (green/blue) to record their stories set in/on/under the sea; for sky (space) stories offer them black paper/card and white chalk/pens. Encourage them to shape their paper with snips/scissors to create wavy, sea-like edges or star/moon/asteroid outlines. Laminate the stories and display them either 'in the sea' (a low, empty/full water tray or paddling pool) or on/from the sky (the ceiling of the setting/classroom). An alternative canvas for their emerging story writing would be on coloured fabric, written using fabric pens.

Story writing 'pick and mix' 2

Here is a second collection of stimulating story writing ideas to engage child authors and enrich professional practices. As explained in 'Story writing "pick and mix" 1' (see p. 23) this assortment of ideas is not attributed to a particular age phase but is offered more as a selection of suggestions for professionals to choose from and adapt in response to the mark making/writing needs of their learners – *put an 'X' by any that you think you might try out!*

X

↓

'Sound' story starters: Offer child authors one-word story starters presented on individual cards e.g. OUCH! ZZZZZZZZ! SPLAT! DING DONG! BEEEEEEEEEP! PLOP! EEEEEEEKKK! GRRRRRRR! Get child authors to initially focus on *what* or *who* is making this noise in their emerging story and *where* the noise is heard.

Special stories: Encourage child authors to write a special emerging story that only *they* will ever read. Offer them stimulating topics or ideas to 'get them started' e.g. *National Kissing Day!*, *The Cupcake Caper!* or *The Day I Fell Out of My Own Body!*, ensuring that what they mark make/write is *for their eyes only*. Provide child authors with individual cardboard writing booths (boxes), invisible ink (see http://tinyurl.com/mw789) and self-adhesive card envelopes to heighten the story's 'specialness'.

Story curiosities: One of Roald Dahl's most prized treasures in his writing hut was his 'cabinet of curiosities' (Sturrock, 2010: 6), a fascinating collection of oddities which may have served as stimuli for his famous children books. Encourage child authors to collect and display interesting and unusual items in the setting/classroom e.g. *bones*, *old kitchen utensils*, *broken clocks* and *toys*, allowing these to be viewed and handled for story inspiration as they mark make/write.

Story wishes: Wishes appear in many children's stories but there is a saying: *Be careful what you wish for!* Get child authors to think about the effects (good and bad) of granted wishes in their own emerging stories, using the story of *The Three Wishes* as a useful structure for adaptation.

Story supporters: Visit http://tinyurl.com/kl4ytnc, reading and reflecting on the practical advice and guidance offered about the role of professionals in supporting young child authors in their story mark making/writing with reference to current curriculum guidance and practical recommendations.

Story edges: Stimulate the visual presentation of child authors' emerging stories by getting them to shape the edge of the paper the story is written on in response to the tale being told e.g. an emerging story set in a castle = ⊓⊔⊓⊔⊓⌐, an emerging story about a lost crown = ⁄\/\/\/\‿, or an emerging story involving characters that live on a bouncy castle = ∿∿∿.

Chapter 3

The plot thickens!

What have you lost?

A universal experience which we can all relate to is losing something or someone: *'Where's Sally's reading book?'*; *'I've misplaced my keys!'*; *'Roger Rabbit is not in his hutch, Mum!'* The inability to find something or someone typically serves as the trigger for a story in which characters go in search for 'the lost'. Work with child authors to consider what is missing in their emerging story – *Shoes? Art work? Treasure? A diary? A tooth?* – and when/where/if/how story characters eventually find it!

Early Years Foundation Stage

* Hide some pens around the setting (both indoors and outdoors). Tell child authors that you have misplaced all of your 'special pens' that you use to write the children's assessments with: *'Can you help me find them, please?'* Invite child authors to mark make/write an emerging story about where they looked and found a pen, *using* the found pen to mark make/write with!
* Get child authors to imagine that something they love e.g. a pet or a teddy bear (think *Where's My Teddy?*) is not there when they get home from the setting: *'Where could he/she be?'* Get child authors to mark make/write an emerging story about the different places that they look, demonstrating their understanding and use of prepositional language (see http://tinyurl.com/o7a8l8w) e.g. **under** *the table*, **behind** *the TV* or **in** *the tumble dryer*.

Key stage 1

* Children typically lose all sorts of things at school e.g. *jumpers, erasers, gloves* and *their homework(!)*. Get child authors to write a 'lost and found' story in which their character loses something and they are told by their teacher to see if it is in the school's lost property box. *'What unusual things do they find in it? Is there something that helps them to find their lost item e.g. a map, a set of directions/prompts or a helpful miniature alien? Is the lost item eventually found? If so, where was it?'*
* Research by Lego Games (Daily Mail, 2012) found that two-thirds of youngsters regularly throw 'a wobbler' [get cross] if they do not win when playing a board game. Invite child authors to actively play board games in class, thinking carefully

about what it *would* feel like or *does* feel like when one of them loses. Challenge them to write an interesting story about what story characters do to ensure the next time they play the game they do not lose. '*How do they do this – cheat? Practice? Rely on luck? Scare the other players?*'

Gold star!

Vandergrift (1997) asserts that it is worth remembering that '[y]oung people are creators as well as consumers of literary works'. Help child authors to *feel* like *real* authors by publishing (displaying) their emerging story mark making/writing on display boards (EYFS) and in class anthologies (KS1). For further ideas see http://tinyurl.com/ye7wf9e and http://tinyurl.com/kddkp43. For practical suggestions as to how to use displays to support emerging story writing in the setting/classroom see http://tinyurl.com/qdzo88d (pp. 2–10).

Family (mis)fortunes!

Many child authors will have heard of, watched and even played the game *Family Fortunes*. Add the prefix 'mis-' and they are likely to generate rich stimuli for their emerging stories; indeed, Despeaux (2012) argues that misfortune can 'make your writing stronger'. The first *Golden Rule of Story Writing* (see http://tinyurl.com/p9a23xl) states: *Don't Bore Your Reader!* With this in mind, challenge child authors to spice up their emerging stories with interesting struggles, encounters, disputes, fights, quarrels and clashes for their families (real/imagined) to endure!

Early Years Foundation Stage

- Encourage child authors to make model houses out of junk materials or construction kits. Get them to imagine that their family have purchased this new house and on the day of moving someone loses the keys: '*How do the family manage to get into the house?*' Support them in mark making/writing an emerging story involving Mummy who gets stuck in the chimney, Wilf the dog who is too big to fit through the cat flap or Baby who tries to clamber through a window!
- Play 'Pass the Parcel', ensuring there are many layers to the package. Get child authors to guess what is in the final layer – *chocolate? Sweets? Keys?* (see the Idea above!) '*What if there was nothing in the final layer – how would different family members react?*' Prompt child authors to role play and then mark make/write an emerging story which includes verbal expressions to reflect how different family members might feel e.g. *WAAAAAAAAAA!* (upset), *Humph!* (fed up), *WHAT!!* (cross) and *NO!* (disappointed).

Key stage 1

- Get child authors to think about family holidays they have been on. *Where did they go? How long did they go for? What did they do on holiday?* Challenge them to retell a holiday tale but add in a rather large source of trouble e.g. *bad weather* or *an approaching asteroid*! '*What do the family do upon hearing the news? How do the family try to break up the asteroid before it reaches the beach? Do they succeed in the nick of time?*'
- Many families like to have 'family time' where they can watch a DVD, play games or just 'chill' together. Get child authors to write a frustrating story when some unwelcome visitors turn up unannounced – think *a crazy wizard*, *an annoying donkey* or *a lonely tramp*. Consider how the visitors disrupt 'family time' and how individual family members try to get rid of their unwanted 'pests' – think about *ignoring them, hiding in the toilet, planning to go out* or *pretending to all be ill at the same time*. '*Do these strategies work?*'

Gold star!

The Golden Rules of Story Writing (see http://tinyurl.com/p9a23xl) offer young child authors and professionals a number of relevant and valuable rules to 'keep in mind' when mark making/writing emerging stories:

1. *Don't Bore Your Reader!*	2. *Be Clear*	3. *Show, Don't Tell*	4. *Be Original*
5. *Get Inside Your Characters' Heads*	6. *Structure Your Story*	7. *Rewrite, Rewrite, Rewrite!*	8. *There Are No Golden Rules*

Use the guidance offered on the website to actively support child authors' mark making/writing, encouraging child authors in upper KS1 to create their *own* rules for story writing (with support) in light of Rule 8 above!

The quest!

Quests are a wonderful plot device for children's stories – they serve as a journey that protagonists go on in search of someone or something, be it tangible e.g. *hidden treasure, money* or '*powerful*' *jewellery* or intangible e.g. *fame, advice* and *love*. Quests typically engage the reader because they involve story characters encountering 'a maze of awe, disappointment, dangers, delays, and experiences' (Durand, 2007) which helps to sustain their interest; this also applies to the child author who decides to mark make/write an emerging story that is driven by a stimulating quest!

Early Years Foundation Stage

- Read *We're Going on a Bear Hunt* (Rosen, 1997). Get child authors to talk about a hunt that *they* would like to go on e.g. a *rabbit/squirrel/penguin/dinosaur* hunt. Support them in mark making/writing an emerging story about this hunt and a key obstacle that they encounter e.g. a sand pit ('*Scritchy Scratchy!*'), a road ('*Zoom Vroom!*') or an icy pond ('*Slip, Skid, CRASH!*'). '*Will you go on this hunt again?*'

- Get child authors to set up different obstacle courses in the outdoor play area. Challenge child authors to try out others' obstacle courses against the clock, awarding golden tickets for perseverance, speed and agility (see http://tinyurl.com/py4p48b). Help them to mark make/write an emerging story about what they had to do to get their golden ticket e.g. *I had ta gw undu a omi net* ('I had to go under an army net.' Tom, 4.10 yrs, gifted).

Key stage 1

- Invite child authors to talk about their personal goals and ambitions: '*What would you like to be when you grow up? What would you like to own?*' Sprinkle child authors with magic 'advancing' dust which allows them to look into the future and 'see' what they have achieved: '*What did you have to do/do you <u>think</u> you had to do to succeed?*' Get them to write about this as a special story for others to learn from e.g. *work hard, stay positive, never give up* and *think big!*
- Talk to child authors about the *Rule of Three* (see http://tinyurl.com/2zkg3z), putting this into context with reference to relevant fairy tales e.g. *The Three Billy Goats Gruff*. Encourage child authors to use this when writing a story involving three obstacles – think *locked doors, bad weather* and *attacking starfish* – that their lead character encounters in their quest to meet the *JibberJabber Jay* so that it is funnier, more satisfying and more effective than just having one obstacle.

Gold star!

Professionals are encouraged to take a look at the following websites, videos and e-book samples about story quests, selecting relevant and applicable academic information and teaching ideas which can be adapted for use with the young child authors in their own settings/classrooms:

Quests: http://tinyurl.com/qyrqo3d	*A Step by Step Guide to Writing Stories with E.R. Reilly!* (video): http://tinyurl.com/qgq64wa
Writing the Hero Quest: http://tinyurl.com/63wa93a	*Story Quest: Creative Writing Guide for Story-Writing Workshops* (e-book sample): http://tinyurl.com/qj5rh3d

What's that you've found?

An interesting way that child authors can develop the plot of their emerging story is by having their lead character find something, be it an inanimate object e.g. *a message in a bottle* or *a sign*, or something living e.g. *a person, a creature* or *an animal*. Their character's 'finding' could be deliberate or it could be by accident, stumbling across it purely by chance. Stimulate child authors' emerging story writing by getting them to be young explorers in the setting/classroom, actively rummaging or foraging about for hidden/surprise items. Alternatively, get them to *imagine* things that their story characters could find, not only in the setting/classroom but in settings outside their place of learning.

Early Years Foundation Stage

- *Easter eggs*. Where were they hidden? How many were found? Who has hidden them there? What is special about the different eggs? What is inside each of them?
- *Ball*. Where was the ball discovered? Who does the ball belong to? What kind of ball is it?
- *Teddy*. Where has Teddy been put? Who has put him there? Why? How does Teddy feel about being put there?
- *Best friend*. Where might he/she be hiding (in a game of hide and seek)? How do you know he/she is hiding there?
- *Whistle*. What does it look like? How big/small is it? What will happen when it is blown?

Key stage 1

- *Key*. What kind of key is it? Who does it belong to? What does the key open/unlock? *A door? A box? An old chest?* Is it best not to use the key?
- *Handwritten note*. What does the note say? Who has written it? When was it written? On what is the message written? What is the message written in? *Chocolate? Felt tip? Blood?*
- *Mouse*. Where has the mouse come from? Is the mouse lost or hiding? Is the mouse looking for food? What does the mouse want to say?
- *Shoe*. What kind of shoe is it? Where is the other shoe? When were the shoes last worn? What is special about the shoes?
- *Photograph*. Who or what is it a picture of? When was it taken? What is the story behind the picture? Does the picture have any special meaning for the person who found it?

When mark making/writing their emerging story, encourage older child authors to think about how their story character reacts when they find something. Are they *surprised? Elated? Scared? Astounded? Glad? Shocked? Intrigued? Joyous? Horrified? Relieved? Thrilled? Puzzled? Excited?* Support able child authors in developing the 'emotional range' of their characters' reactions by making reference to visual emotion charts (facial expressions), online word lists or using 'emotions' dice, spinners, photographs and puppets (see Fox and Lentini, 2006). *'What do characters do with "the found" once they have found it?'*

Gold star!

In *Lost and Found* (Jeffers, 2005) the penguin finds friendship in the boy. Help young child authors to recognise things that their characters could find that are not tangible e.g. *companionship, the truth, one's voice, happiness, inner courage, love, strength of character, peace* and *faith.* With support, encourage child authors to consider how their lead character(s) could 'find' these non-tangible entities through their experiences and encounters with other individuals, be they both positive and not so positive.

Open sesame!

There are many stories which involve characters opening something – think *letters (The Jolly Postman), a parcel (No Problem!)* and *jars of honey (Winnie the Pooh).* The repercussions of doing this typically help to 'fuel the plot' (Hadley-Garcia, 2013) and satisfy the reader's curiosity with regard to finding out what is inside! Encourage child authors to weave into their emerging story an object or item which is opened (see examples below), reminding them to think about what happens as a result of these objects/items being opened!

Early Years Foundation Stage

* *Jack-in-the-box.* What/who could pop out instead of 'Jack'? *A rabbit? 'Jill'? A monster?*
* *Gift* – birthday/Christmas. What is given? Does the recipient like it? Why/not?
* *Pass the parcel.* What is the prize when the last layer is unwrapped? *A mirror? Lego? Fish?!*
* *Big cardboard box.* What is inside? *A TV?* Who's hiding inside? *Mummy? Grandpa? Friends?*
* *Envelope.* What size/shape is it? What's inside? *A musical card? Photographs? Drawings?*
* *Chest.* What's inside when the chest is unlocked? *Sweets? Toys? Dressing-up clothes? Treasure? Their best friend? A pet?*

Key stage 1

* *Door.* Who is 'revealed' as the door slowly opens? *A princess? A bully? An alien? A hippo?*
* *Bottle* – medicine/water/pop/baby. What happens to characters that smell/drink the vapours/liquids inside it?
* *Book.* What's inside the cut-out pages? *A map? A torch? A note? Instructions? Money?*
* *Bag.* What jumps out when the bag is unzipped? *A kitten? A squirrel? A crocodile?*

- *Fridge.* Who is sat there on the shelf when the fridge is opened? *Teddy? Doggie? Olly the orange?* Who is found hiding in the defrosting ice box? *Ice Baby? Snuffles the hamster?*
- *Wardrobe.* What/who falls out when the wardrobe is opened? *Snow? Old clothing? Dora the Explorer? Katie Morag?*

Support child authors in making their emerging story a surprising experience by adding simple pop-up paper features to their illustrations, thus enhancing the 'reveal' aspect of their object/item. See Irvine (2005) for practical ideas on how to increase the complexity of the paper engineering depending on the abilities of child authors (and the confidence of professionals!).

Gold star!

Visit http://tinyurl.com/now2shc for a wonderful PDF full of Foldables by Zike (2008). Consider the potential of using these with child authors to stimulate their emerging story writing e.g. encouraging child authors to mark make/write their emerging stories on differently designed Foldables (pp. 8–9). Alternatively, visit http://tinyurl.com/6e9podx or http://tinyurl.com/ps7qjzj for further ideas and suggestions in relation to story writing which can be adapted for the child authors you work with.

The fear factor!

Roddy (2003: 3) advocates the three-step method of 'a tangible Objective, some Obstacles and the Outcome' to help child authors 'shape a story idea into a finished narrative'. An obstacle that almost everyone can relate to is that of fears (*feeling afraid*) and phobias (*intense levels of fear*). There are many things that can frighten us and these offer child authors a real 'wealth of possibility' when thinking about what their story character's fear or phobia is (*the obstacle*), what their *objective* is (to face or overcome their fear or phobia perhaps?) and how they try to overcome it, the *outcome* being whether they succeed or not.

Early Years Foundation Stage

- During circle time opportunities invite child authors to identify things that frighten them e.g. *the dark, loud noises* or *strangers*. Get them to mark make/write an emerging story about ways that they try to 'cope' with these fears e.g. *squeeze Teddy tight, hold Mummy's hand* or *sleep with the light on*. Stress to them that everyone get scared and that it is nothing to be ashamed of.
- Sensitively show child authors pictures or video footage of snakes, spiders, rodents and dogs. *Which one are they most scared of?* Encourage them to talk about what alarms them about these animals, providing 'safe' ways to help them overcome their phobia e.g. *looking at books, playing with toy animals* or *handling sensory materials similar to the animal's skin*. Invite them to mark make/write an emerging story of how they have tried to/succeeded in overcoming their fear or phobia.

Key stage 1

- Young children typically have a fear of imaginary things such as trolls, ghosts, monsters and ghouls. Encourage them to write a 'tables-turned' story in which it is the trolls, ghosts, monsters and ghouls that are frightened of them! '*What does this prevent them from doing? Where do they go and hide?*' Suggest that child authors read their completed story to themselves at bedtime as a funny reminder that everyone/every*thing* gets scared!
- Smith *et al.* (2014) suggest that one phobia type relates to the natural environment: '[F]ear of heights...storms...water, and...the dark.' Suggest that child authors identify a setting where their story character would come face to face with one of these phobias, building up written descriptions of their *physical* reactions to it in their story e.g. 'difficulty breathing...racing or pounding heart...chest pain or tightness...trembling or shaking...feeling dizzy or lightheaded...a churning stomach...hot or cold flashes...tingling sensations [or] sweating'. '*What happens next?*'

Gold star!

Soar Higher (2006: 1) proposes a technique called SOAR to help people develop accomplishment stories that can be told to showcase their skills in interview situations. This can easily be adapted to offer 'structural support' for young child authors when verbalising/mark making/writing their emerging stories:

SOAR stories	Story mark making/writing using SOAR
Situation: Describe the situation.	**Situation:** Talk/mark make/write about the 'story situation' e.g. who is in your story and where it takes place.
Obstacles: Describe the obstacles you faced.	**Obstacles:** Talk/mark make/write about the obstacle(s) your character faces.
Actions: List the actions you took.	**Actions:** Talk/mark make/write about the actions of your character in response to the obstacle(s) they face.
Results: Describe the results you helped obtain and the benefits to your organisation.	**Results:** Talk/mark make/write about the results of your character's actions and the benefits of these to themselves and others.

Model the use of this to help young child authors see the value of using SOAR to help them structure their emerging written stories.

Rescue me!

Dictionary definitions of the verb 'to rescue' emphasise the idea of setting free or saving someone or something from danger, attack, imprisonment or death. 'The rescue' is a common plotline in stories and films and is typically characterised by the hero rescuing the damsel in distress – think *Superman* saving Lois Lane or Prince

Phillip rescuing *Sleeping Beauty* with a kiss. Child authors can use 'the rescue' as a stimulating driving force for their own emerging story, particularly as they can be creative with regard to *who* or *what* is going to be rescued and *how* and *why* the rescue takes place.

Early Years Foundation Stage

- Place soft toys all around the outdoor play area. Invite child authors to play the role of the Toy Rescuer. *'Can you find the toys and save them before it rains?'* Encourage them to mark make/write an emerging story about how they rescued a particular toy e.g. 'I went up the ladder to get Kittycat' (story dictation, Sab, 3.9 yrs).
- Read children's stories involving *Fireman Sam* or *The Rescue Princesses* who always 'come to the rescue'. Support child authors in becoming *Firegirl Tammy* or *The Rescue Prince* by getting dressed up in appropriate clothing, encouraging them to mark make/write an emerging story about someone or something that they save e.g. *Grandma from a hailstorm* or *Harry the hamster from Brian, the angry dog*.

Key stage I

- Show child authors images of individuals who work in the three main emergency services – police, fire and emergency medical (ambulances). Encourage child authors to mark make/write a simple story about a character (human/animal) who is rescued by one of these services: *'How are they rescued? Is it an easy/difficult rescue? Why/not? How are individuals rewarded for their actions?'*
- Offer child authors the story title *'Captain Kaloney to the Rescue!'* Work with child authors as a whole class to thought shower ideas as to who Captain Kaloney is, what he/she looks like, and who/what is going to be rescued e.g. *friends*, *family members* or *their teacher(!)*. Invite child authors to write their own version of the rescue story in response to the title, considering where their story is to take place: *Space? An aeroplane? A boat?*

Gold star!

Create a series of rescue prompts (words or images presented on individual cards) to help those child authors who require some inspiration to 'kick-start' their thinking with regard to mark making/writing their rescue story. Examples might include:

Lost	*Flood*	*Chains*	*Shark*	*Trapped*
Fire	*Illness*	*Storm*	*Pit*	*Dungeon*
Ghost	*Kidnap*	*Spaceship*	*Plane*	*Prison*
Tree	*Lock*	*Train*	*Magic spell*	*Kiss*
Criminal	*Evil Doctor*	*Tied up*	*Fall*	*Broken*

Fight	Pipe	Dragon	Dinosaur	Sinking Ship
Alien	Car	Cave	Bully	Cage
Witch	Explosion	Bus	Blind-folded	Cliff edge
Hole	Battle	Well	Cell	Wizard

Other rescue prompt cards can be created by older child authors themselves in response to their talk about/reading of rescue stories (those in fiction books or reported in the news).

Didn't I warn you?

The 'warning story', as Corbett (2008c) explains, follows a simple pattern: '[T]he tale hinges on a warning being ignored.' This clearly guides the plot of the film *Gremlins* where the strict instructions of the Chinese shop owner – *do not expose Gizmo, the lovable Mogwai, to bright light, get him wet or feed him after midnight* – are overlooked with disastrous results! Encourage child authors to use their own experiences to fuel their emerging warning stories, particularly as *'Didn't I warn you?'* is likely to be something they have heard many a time from parents/carers and professionals 'after-the-event'!

Early Years Foundation Stage

• Share with child authors a range of different *'Didn't I warn you?'* comments e.g. *'Didn't I warn you not to forget to push your chair under the table?', 'Didn't I warn you not to go outside without your jacket?'* or *'Didn't I warn you not to hold the paint pot on its side?'* Get child authors to think about why professionals might say these things, mark making/writing an emerging story which explains what happens when these warnings (or others) are ignored. *'What will you do next time?'*

• Read *Warning: Do Not Open This Book!* (Lehrhaupt, 2013). Encourage child authors to create a sample story page of a new version of the book with relevant mark making/writing/drawings, replacing the mischievous monkeys with an animal of their choosing: *What kind of havoc do* they *cause when the page is opened?*

Key stage 1

• Challenge child authors to collaboratively identify dangerous places in the local area e.g. 'car dumps, a quarry, a cliff or an old tin mine' (Corbett, 2008b). Invite them to select one, writing a story which explains the reasons why this place is dangerous and what unfortunately happens to one (or more) of their story characters when they fail to take account of the verbal warning given to them by a parent/carer, family member or the 'mystery voice'. *'Who rescues them? How are they rescued? Are they rescued "in the nick of time"?'*

- Read *Do Not Open This Book!* (Cowley, 1998). Encourage child authors to rewrite the story, creating their own warning title e.g. *Stop Reading This! Close This Book, I Say! Look No Further! Put The Book Down NOW!* with a new lead character and an amusing, surprise ending. *'What/who is the big "reveal"?'*

Gold star!

The 'warning tales' of the Brothers Grimm – think *Little Red Riding Hood* and *Hansel and Gretel* – have both delighted (and frightened) children for over 200 years. Using NBC's police drama series *Grimm* as the inspiration for this idea, work with child authors to modernise select fairy tales for the twenty-first-century reader with reference to up-to-date fashions (e.g. hoodies), music (R&B), popular culture (taking a selfie) and technology (Wi-Fi and iPads). Alternatively, see Robinson (2005) for some 'mixed up' inspiration!

Making mistakes!

Cleaver (2006: 22) claims that a useful 'plot trigger' for a story involves a character making a mistake. Children's story titles such as *Big Dog and Little Dog Make a Mistake*, *Snake's Mistake* and *The Fairy's Mistake* highlight how errors serve as an effective catalyst for an interesting emerging story. Encourage child authors to initially talk about mistakes that *they* have personally made, either at home or in the setting/at school. Create a verbal/written list of these so that they can be used to stimulate their own and others' emerging stories. Possible examples include:

Early Years Foundation Stage

- Calling their teacher/friend by the wrong name.
- Counting out objects incorrectly.
- Picking up and putting on the wrong jacket.
- Accidently pushing past a peer or friend and hurting them.
- Wrongly accusing someone of taking their snack/milk.
- Putting their picture in the wrong book bag.
- Answering a question incorrectly.

Key stage 1

- Not listening to the instructions given out.
- Leaving one's lunchbox at home on the kitchen table.
- Not thinking before opening their mouth and speaking.
- Telling untruths (fibs).
- Forgetting where something has been put/left.
- Putting something back in the wrong place.
- Saying words in the wrong order in a sentence.

Berkun (2005) suggests there are four *types* of mistakes that people make, a couple of which are appropriate for young child authors to be aware of:

- *stupid* [silly] e.g. stubbing a toe (apt for EYFS);
- *simple* e.g. having the electricity go out in the middle of a party because Dad forgot to pay the bill (apt for KS1);
- *involved* (mistakes that are understood but require effort to prevent) e.g. regularly arriving late to school every day; and
- *complex* (mistakes that have complicated causes and no obvious way to avoid next time) e.g. relationships with others (friends, family members, girl/boyfriends) that fail.

Use the above to help child authors to categorise the different mistakes they decide to mark make/write about. Through focused taught input ensure that child authors appreciate that *everyone makes mistakes* – it is part of being a human being! This also applies to the characters in their emerging stories – readers will find protagonists who never make any mistakes 'too perfect' and rather boring. It is therefore important for characters to not only *make* a mistake(s) but also try to *rectify* their wrong doing(s). This might involve them:

Sincerely apologising for what they did/said	Offering some penitence e.g. being upset or writing letters of apology
Taking responsibility for their actions and admitting they made a mistake	Putting in place practical strategies to ensure that mistakes do not happen again

Adapted from Cottringer (2005)

Talk with child authors during carpet time or PHSCE opportunities about practical ways that they can rectify mistakes they make in their work and their relationships with others to support their emerging story writing e.g. *be honest, listen to what others have to say, try harder next time, act on your errors, double check things, avoid situations where easy mistakes are made, concentrate and don't rush* and *think before you act*. Bring these strategies alive through the use of role play and drama (see http://tinyurl.com/owgmult (EYFS) and http://tinyurl.com/nh8uufj (KS1)).

Gold star!

In *The Girl Who Never Made Mistakes* (Pett and Rubinstein, 2012), Beatrice Bottomwell learns that it is not possible to be perfect all the time. Help child authors to develop their emerging story endings by encouraging them to mark make/write about the 'lessons learned' by their characters from the mistakes that they make e.g. *not to do 'X' again, always put a coat on when it is raining, think before you speak, take your time* or *never laugh at others' misfortune!*

Story writing 'pick and mix' 3

Here is a third collection of stimulating story writing ideas to engage child authors and enrich professional practices. As explained in 'Story writing "pick and mix" 1' (see p. 23) this assortment of ideas is not attributed to a particular age phase but is offered more as a selection of suggestions for professionals to choose from and adapt in response to the mark making/writing needs of their learners – *put an 'X' by any that you think you might try out!*

X

	Story preparations: Virtually all of the planning and preparations for child authors' actual emerging story writing is usually done in the setting/classroom – suggest that they 'Parent/Carer-Plan' at home with their (step)mother/father/carer (over dinner perhaps), talking about the emerging story that they intend to mark make/write. *Might parents/carers have some ideas to help enrich their (step)child's tale?* Develop a parent/carer support guidance sheet with useful pointers/questions so that they can successfully support their child.
	Story shorts: Get child authors to mark make/write emerging 'tiny' stories on Post-It notes, scraps of paper or small paper pieces. Gather these up and get child authors to select one, drawing pictures/talking/mark making/writing about what they think happens next in the story.
	Story swirls: Encourage child authors to 'swirl spot' while looking through Sidman's (2011) book *Swirl by Swirl: Spirals in Nature.* Invite them to mark make/write an emerging story on spiral-shaped paper involving one of the spotted swirls that relate to different animals e.g. *hedgehogs, sea horses* and *elephants.*
	Bingo ball stories: Invest in a toy bingo ball machine which can used to help child authors choose stimulating story ideas available at http://tinyurl.com/88j7z8m by counting down the list in response to the number selected. Adapt suggestions to meet the needs and abilities of different child authors.
	Story schooling: Professionals who remember the defunct *National Literacy Strategy* (DfEE, 1998) and the *Primary National Strategy* (DfES, 2003) may recall the three advocated methods of teaching children writing: • *Shared* Writing (writing *with* children); • *Guided* Writing (writing *by* children); and • *Independent* Writing (writing *on their own*). Continue to utilise these powerful teaching strategies along with *modelled* writing (professional writing *for* children) to effectively support learning in the setting/classroom (see http://tinyurl.com/kd4qprr for further details).
	Story about a story: Challenge child authors to mark make/write an emerging story about a child author who decides to write a story. *'What happens to them during the writing e.g. are they disturbed by a constant stream of telephone calls, door bells, alarm clocks, noisy pets, crying babies and loud music? Do they ever complete their story?'*
	Story books: Make child authors feel like real authors by getting them to mark make/write their stories in different kinds of paper books. Visit http://tinyurl.com/qzll2r3 and http://tinyurl.com/lq3uytx (pp. 13–48) for a collection of adaptable ideas.

Chapter 4

Colourful conflict!

It's all in my mind!

One of the two main types of conflict in story is *internal conflict*. Sometimes referred to as *self-* or *intrapersonal conflict*, it describes the struggle that takes place in a character's mind. This is evident in the verbalised thoughts of Charlie Brown in the comic strip *Peanuts*: 'I feel terrible! I hate myself!!' (see Rubin, 2012). Support child authors in developing their use of internal conflict in their emerging story mark making/writing, revealing this through their use of 'dialogue, narration and a character's actions' (Hickman, 2014) with support when making difficult choices or decisions.

Early Years Foundation Stage

- Support child authors in identifying times when they have been tempted to take something which does not belong to them e.g. *toys, cupcakes, pencils* or *money*. Get them to mark make/write an emerging story about what they wanted to take, adding a reason for not taking them e.g. *It's wrong! It's naughty! Stealing is bad!*
- Show child authors an old broken toy: '*I wonder who broke it/how it got broken?*' Talk to child authors about why we struggle to admit when we have done something wrong for fear of getting into trouble. Encourage them to mark make/write an emerging story about a character being scared to confess they kicked/stole/ate/hid/dropped/smashed/lost/ripped something, talking as they work about how it is always good to 'own up' rather than say 'I didn't do it!'

Key stage 1

- During circle time encourage child authors to share their experiences of feeling guilty e.g. *saying 'No!' to a request made by Mum, eating too much chocolate* or *not sharing their toys with a sibling*. Use one of these experiences as the basis for a truth-informed story (one where the author is honest about their feelings), changing the characters' names. '*How did you effectively deal with this guilt?*'
- Everybody at one time or another lacks confidence in themselves e.g. *talking to someone new, asking for help* or *putting their hand up to answer a question*. Suggest that child authors write an interesting story about the internal struggle a character experiences before the 'opening night' of a school performance,

competing in the Sports Day or sitting a music exam. *'How do they positively handle their feelings? Do they succeed?'*

Gold star!

Gold star! suggestions usually offer professionals a single, quality idea; this one offers 30! Visit http://tinyurl.com/nbyeh9 for 'a variety of eclectic, classroom-tested techniques' related to the teaching of writing taken from full-length articles published by the *National Writing Project* in America. Personal favourites include Ideas 8, 10 and 20. Consider ways of adapting these techniques to suit the age group/needs of those that you work with.

Intense illnesses and injuries!

Baudet (2013) asserts that a '[c]haracter against illness, [be it a] parent, friend or self' serves as an interesting *external* form of conflict. All child authors will experience some form of real-life illness (a cough or a cold) or injury (a bruised elbow or a 'bumped' head). With support they can draw on this to help them mark make/write a stimulating emerging story which *could* (hint hint!) explore the challenges that characters must confront, manage and (hopefully) overcome when they or others are poorly/injured.

Early Years Foundation Stage

*   Get child authors to sensitively talk about their experiences of being unwell e.g. *having a poorly tummy, a sore finger* or *a runny nose*. Encourage them to draw or paint a 'story scene' of what they did to make themselves feel better e.g. *hug Mummy/Teddy, have a nap* or *watch TV*. Assist them in adding marks/writing to their story scene for others to read, enjoy and learn from.
*   Use first-aid resources from the Doctor's Surgery role play area such as bandages, wipes and plasters as valuable stimuli for an emerging story in which child authors mark make/write about a family member, their 'injury issue' and what is done to 'help them heal' e.g. *Dab cut hiz fin gu Mum put a pas tr on it*. ('Dad cut his finger. Mum put a plaster on it.' Hollie, 4.11 yrs, unaided.)

Key stage 1

*   Read *Little Red Riding Hood* (Gordon, 2013). Get child authors to consider why Grandma might be unwell. *'Does she have toothache or a fever?'* Suggest they include this in their own *adapted* retelling of the story, exploring what is inside *Big Blue* Riding Hood's *bicycle* basket that will help *Grandpa Joe* feel better e.g. *tablets, syrups, lozenges* or *ointments* (examples suggested by Joe, 6.4 yrs).
*   Take child authors onto the playground area and get them to think about/discuss/role play ways that they could accidentally hurt themselves there e.g. *stumble and graze their knee* or *twist and sprain their ankle*. Consider ways that

story characters could avoid the above during a 'playtime marathon', writing a short story which describes simple preventative strategies that they take to fully enjoy the extended playtime period e.g. *avoid walking on ice, keep an eye out for big kids* or *stretch before running*.

Gold star!

Morris (2013) claims music to be 'an odd facilitator for writing'. Offer child authors access to a range of different genres of *sound stimuli* (see http://tinyurl.com/najmfqy) in the setting/classroom, either *before* they mark make/write (e.g. listening to 'The Aquarium' from *The Carnival of the Animals* by Saint-Saëns prior to mark making/writing an emerging story set under the sea), *during* their story mark making/writing (e.g. new-age music – think Robert Haig Coxon – to inspire and relax child authors), or after they have written (as part of the discussing/rereading/redrafting process as/if appropriate).

Competitive streak!

Cantador and Conde (2010: 1) suggest that '[i]t is controversial whether competition in education is positive or not'. While there are fors and againsts for its use, competitions serve as a rich source of conflict to stimulate emerging story mark making/writing – see *I Want to Win!* (Ross, 2012). With trials suggesting that introducing a competitive edge to school mealtimes could increase the number of children eating fruit and vegetables by a third (see Belot *et al.*, 2014), it may be possible to raise engagement and quality levels of emerging story mark making/writing in the setting/classroom by a third by weaving a competitive streak into the 'story mix'!

Early Years Foundation Stage

- Show child authors a pair of new 'magic' trainers (picture/real). Tell them that the wearer can run faster than any land animal on the planet. Suggest that they draw a picture of 'fast' animals at the start line of a running race (think *cheetahs, antelopes, hares* and *greyhounds*) alongside themselves wearing the trainers. *'Just how fast can story characters run in them?'* ('Really fast, weeeeeeeee!' Story dictation, Dinah, 4.0 yrs.)
- Set up an engaging obstacle course in the outdoor play area. Encourage child authors to attempt to complete the course in the quickest time possible. Invite them to mark make/write an emerging story about competing against one of their friends in the setting. *'Who wins? Why do they win? Does it matter who wins – are you still the best of friends?'*

Key stage 1

- Introduce child authors to the notion of a 'Spelling Bee' (see http://tinyurl.com/qxnstu6). Provide opportunities for child authors to compete with others in class in a mock Spelling Bee role play situation. Use this as the basis for a piece of fictitious story writing in which unusual story characters such as *clowns, knights, dancers* or *talking cats* 'do battle' using words that child authors are learning that week. '*Who becomes the reigning champion and what is the winning word that only they can spell?*'

- Visit http://tinyurl.com/6leuk, encouraging child authors to think about the true meaning of *Red Nose Day* (other charities and events are available). Invite them to write a funny story which involves a competition between individuals trying to raise the most money for charity by doing funny things e.g. *a Singing-Songs-Backwards karaoke event, wearing all their clothes inside out, only eating red things for the day* or *a sponsored shower-off!* '*Who raises the most cash? How much is raised? What is done with the money collected?*'

Gold star!

Dough Disco is described by Bennett (2014: 4) as

> a daily activity which combines the use of pieces of dough with a series of hand and finger exercises. These strengthen and develop children's fine and gross motor dexterity, hand-eye co-ordination, proprioception [the body's ability to sense movement within joints and joint position], balance, low load control, grip and most importantly, their self-esteem!

Visit http://tinyurl.com/q63r4yj to see Shonette Bason energetically demonstrating her Dough Disco concept! Ideal for child authors in the EYFS, consider ways to adapt this for child authors, particularly boys in KS1 (Wilson, 2013) who are 'pained' by writing, in terms of the movements made, the music selected and the material to manipulate!

Antagonistic animals!

It is well argued that conflict is essential to plot as without it there would *be* no plot (Brownhill, 2013)! A common form of external conflict present in children's stories is that of 'man versus man' e.g. *two rival female football teams battling it out for the Golden Cup*. 'Man versus man' does not just mean human beings; animals can serve as a living form of conflict – think *Rikki-Tikki-Tavi* (Kipling and Davis, 1992). With this in mind, invite child authors to thought shower all of the animals they know with drawn sketches and/or words, select one and 'consider the conflict' that they could present to fuel a super emerging story!

Early Years Foundation Stage

- Get child authors to imagine it is World Animal Day and Mummy or Daddy has decided that they can go to the pet shop and choose a new pet (use stuffed toys as part of the role play). Support them in mark making/writing an emerging story about the difficulties of introducing a non-house-trained pet into their home – think *chewing the furniture, running away* and *wee-weeing on the carpet!*

- Sensitively talk to child authors about animals that frighten them: *'What is it about them that scares you?'* e.g. *they growl, bite, hiss* or *scratch*. Get them to mark make/write an emerging story about how they try to overcome their fear when faced with one of these animals e.g. *stand firm, keep their hands to themselves, shout 'No!'* or *ignore them. 'Does it work?'*

Key stage 1

- Initiate a discussion with child authors about different animal shows and competitions with reference to web-based images or the story *Katie Morag and the Two Grandmothers* (Hedderwick, 2010). Challenge them to write a competitive story in which they decide to take their pet (real/imagined) to try and win some rosettes but their pet's behaviour on the day causes humorous turmoil for everyone in attendance – think *chasing after the other animals, not sitting still for the photograph* or *refusing to jump/fly through the hoop*!
- Support child authors in identifying animals that are skittish or shy – think *mice, deer, chipmunks, foxes, kittens* and *squirrels*. Suggest that they write a story about going to a zoo full of nervous animals armed with their digital cameras but not 'snapping' a single animal. *'What do you end up taking pictures of instead?'*

Gold star!

Download the PDF at http://tinyurl.com/o63uscv which offers a series of conflict bookmarks that can be used by professionals to help child authors build up their understanding of different types of conflict when reading published stories and the written work of their peers. Consider adapting these for younger child authors through the use of pictures and images, space for drawings, tick lists, questions, prompts and visual reminders. For other bookmarks that can be used to promote active reading, letter formation practice, spelling 'tests' and literacy-based gifts for Mothers'/Fathers' Day see http://tinyurl.com/n5umw7n.

Technological turbulence!

It is argued that conflict 'must exist for the story to exist' (see http://tinyurl.com/pvrqca3, p. 1). This 'makes the story move' (p. 1) and one source of conflict to assure this movement comes in the form of technology. This appears in a lot of science fiction stories and cartoons – think *Robot* (Pienkowski, 1981), *Metal Mickey* on TV and *Transformers* (cartoon and films). When child authors 'place...a character against man-made entities which may possess "artificial intelligence"' (p. 2) – think *machines, robots, gadgets* and *computers* – rich story potential then exists (see Beaty, 2013; Gall, 2013).

Early Years Foundation Stage

- Provide child authors with digital cameras for them to take images of the setting. When looking at the images or printing out the pictures secretly switch the memory card or print out some different images: *'Are these the pictures that you took?'* Get child authors to mark make/write about the mischievous digital camera/printer, considering why they are 'misbehaving' e.g. *they are bored/tired/being deliberately naughty* or *think that it is funny.*

- Offer child authors a remote control (toy/real). Tell them that it is a magic remote: *'What do you think it operates?'* Get them to explore the setting, generating creative ideas with regards to what it operates e.g. *flushes the toilet, makes a paint brush paint a picture* or *opens the shed in the outdoor play area.* Support child authors in committing one of their ideas down on paper as an emerging story. Think *Click* (the Adam Sandler film) as inspiration.

Key stage I

- Show child authors select scenes from the film *Chitty Chitty Bang Bang* which show Pott's inventions in the kitchen (see http://tinyurl.com/pogl2qw: 1.32 mins+). Invite child authors to invent a new machine to help them at home e.g. *a clothes folding device, a homework writing arm* or *a bed-making robot.* *'What happens when the machine goes wrong?'* Get child authors to write a 'funny short', considering how they have to right the wrong doings of their machine before Mum finds out!
- Show child authors images (web-based) of different laptops. Get child authors to think about different ways a laptop could become a nuisance for its user e.g. *tries to 'snap' typing fingers, changes the letters around on the keyboard* or *refuses to be switched on.* Help child authors to write these ideas into a rebus story [one which uses pictures to represent words or parts of words] (see http://tinyurl.com/26m4fa4 as an example), replacing individual words in the tale with hand-drawn/digital images.

Gold star!

Horn (n.d.: 1) argues that: '[L]earning the role of view point and understanding that each person has a unique point of view (POV) is one of the most important thinking skills that a child can acquire.' Read Horn's interesting article on POV and the PDF that is available at http://tinyurl.com/l8o7quz, using role play and oral questions (EYFS) and POV stories and video clips (KS1) to help child authors learn how to link the events in a story causally (Emery, 1996).

Wild weather!

Jones (2014) claims that the '[w]eather has played an important role in many military operations throughout history. The timing of the D-Day invasion [for example] was heavily influenced by weather forecasts and conditions.' This 'important role' is also evident in many well-known stories – think *The Rainy Day* (rain) or *The Wizard of Oz* (tornado). With a wealth of weathers available to choose from, child authors should be encouraged to use the weather to stimulate their written emerging stories.

Early Years Foundation Stage

- Encourage child authors to play in the outdoor area during different weather conditions e.g. when it is *windy, snowy, rainy* or *sunny*. Support them in mark making/writing an emerging story about what they like to do in their favourite 'play weather', collating their thoughts in a group, weather-shaped book (for ideas see Howard and Cigrand, 2003).
- There are several story books about different animals 'in the snow' e.g. *Tiger in the Snow!* (Butterworth, 2006) and *Foxes in the Snow* (Emmett, 2010). Invite child authors to put *their* favourite animal in this snowy situation. *'What do they get up to in the fluffy whiteness?'* Mark make/write about their adventures in an emerging story presented on large paper using snowballs (cotton-wool balls) as mark making/writing implements with chalk dust or white paint.

Key stage 1

- Challenge child authors to write a short story using personified weather as the central character e.g. *Crying Cloud, Frightened Fog* or *Lonely Lightning*. Work with them to establish why they are crying/frightened/lonely and if/how they change by the end of the story e.g. *Lonely Lightning makes friends with the Lightning Bolts* (a weather-based sports team).
- Many people enjoy the sun when they go on holiday in the summer. *'What if the sun decided to take his holiday during the summer season? Where would he go? What would he do? Who would he go with? Who would replace the sun?'* Suggest that child authors write their engaging story on yellow circular paper, presenting their story sentences on an Archimedean spiral line.

Gold star!

Help child authors to quickly recognise high frequency words (EYFS) and build their levels of accuracy when learning 'word family' spellings (KS1) by presenting words with the initial and final letters written in a different colour e.g. **r**a**p**; **d**readfu**l**. Also visit http://tinyurl.com/pufrg9g for information, resources and links to 'a fun system' called *Rainbow Words* to support their learning of letters/sounds, sight word recognition and spellings, all of which can be used to support them when engaging in story mark making/writing.

Challenging environments!

A key source of external conflict in story comes in the form of the physical environment. This is supported by the Balance Publishing Company (1989: 1) who define 'Man against Nature' as 'a character [who] struggles with the elements'. Exemplification of this can be found in the work of London (2013: 1) where the protagonist 'wants to live, but Nature, in the form of the barren Arctic tundra, stands in his way. To survive, he must overcome all that Nature puts in his way: an injured ankle, hunger, cold, distance, wolves, etc.' *What interesting challenges can the environment throw at story characters in the hands of your child authors, I wonder?*

Early Years Foundation Stage

- Teach/sing the nursery rhyme 'The Grand Old Duke of York' (see http://tinyurl.com/l3nx3n5). Let child authors experience the difficulties of climbing up a steep hill using sloped mats and raised planks on boxes in the outdoor play area. Invite child authors to mark make/write an emerging story about how they did/would try to overcome this challenge e.g. *go around the hill, jump over it on enormous springs* or *dig a tunnel through it.*
- Read *We're Roaming in the Rainforest* (Krebs, 2011). Invite child authors to roam the dark forest floor of the 'rainforest' (the setting), being on the lookout with torches for dangerous animals (stuffed toys) e.g. *jaguars, elephants, tigers* and *gorillas. 'What would you do if one of them tried to attack you?'* Get them to mark make/write down an emerging story about this 'attack' and how they would protect themselves e.g. *shout at it, hit it with a stick* or *catch it in a net.*

Key stage I

- Show child authors images of the polar regions (Arctic and Antarctic). Offer them a small rucksack, getting them to fill it with resources from the classroom that they could use to keep themselves warm. Invite them to write a story that describes any creative ways they could keep warm e.g. *sleep by the* Human Torch or *'I put coton wul up me nows to stop me brayn frezing.'* (Darren, 5.8 yrs, independent writing.)
- Play the theme tune from the film *Lawrence of Arabia* (see http://tinyurl.com/lg48e9u) as child authors think about and write a story about the challenges that the desert presents to story characters when they go there on an 'undiscovered' adventure holiday e.g. *lack of shelter, extreme heat* and *sandstorms. 'What could your protagonists invent/create to help them overcome these challenges?'* Encourage older child authors to explore *The Famous Five's Survival Guide* (Blyton, 2008) for any useful ideas!

Gold star!

Maynes and Julien-Schultz (2011: 194) argue that graphic '[o]rganizers provide cognitive structures that support learners' ability to relate ideas and support critical thinking and higher levels of cognition'. Visit http://tinyurl.com/nej548t, considering how the graphic organisers presented on pp. 4–8 could be used to make 'abstract concepts more concrete' for older child authors to think/write about in their emerging stories e.g. *time, being free, good and evil, love* and *success.* Alternatively, use these to help child authors develop an understanding of story structure – think the *Story Mountain*!

Forces of nature!

Man versus nature is considered to be one of the most basic forms of conflict in a story. This 'nature' can be on a small scale (think Rosen's (1997) *swirling-whirling snowstorm*) or a large one (think of the flood in the biblical story of Noah and the Ark; see Cousins, 2013). The challenge for child authors is to purposefully put their story characters in a situation where they come face to face with a natural disaster influenced by Mother Nature! *But which disaster to choose from* (see http://tinyurl.com/l5lbhk) *and what happens next...?*

Early Years Foundation Stage

- Encourage child authors to take inspiration when they are in the sunny outdoor play area, mark making/writing about the onset of a heat wave. *'What exciting things could you get up to in the hot sunshine? Play in the paddling pool? Have a picnic in the shade? Lick a multicoloured ice-lolly?'* Mark make/write their emerging story using water and paintbrushes on the outdoor play area walls/floor, capturing their emerging story with a digital camera before it evaporates!
- Offer child authors paper shaped like lightning bolts. Invite them to mark make/write on it an emerging story involving 'lightning' associated characters e.g. Bolt the dog (see Disney's *Bolt*), Lightning McQueen (see Pixar's *Cars*) or Leo (the Lightning Bug – see Drachman, 2003). *'What happens to them during a thunderous lightning storm? Do they get scared?'*

Key stage I

- Show child authors a picture of a busy seaside scene. Give them time to 'take in' the different things they can see going on. *'Now...imagine that a "swirling, whirling"* <u>sand</u>*storm suddenly rips right across the beach – what do people in the scene do?'* Invite child authors to write about what happens in the form of a frantic story in which characters' survival instincts see them creatively trying to shield themselves from the sandstorm using lilos, towels and umbrellas.
- Show child authors the volcano eruption scene from Disney's film *Fantasia* (see http://tinyurl.com/k2avr8c: from 3.04 mins). Suggest that they write a stimulating story involving other characters from the film e.g. the Dancing Hippos or Yin Sed the sorcerer who accidentally get caught up in the eruption: *'How do they manage to survive it? Through the use of magical spells? Visiting superheroes? Prayer? A rocket? A magma-repelling body suit?'*

Gold star!

The use of varied writing paper, in terms of its colour and shape, can be stimulating and performance improving for child authors (see Winter and Winter, 2009: 3). Continually offer them paper of different hues, tints, shades and tones (see http://tinyurl.com/3mmvqj2 for information) which can be shaped by professionals or child authors in response to key aspects of their emerging story e.g. objects (*paper shaped into an open box*), settings (*a dome to represent a character who lives in the* Eden Project) or characters (*paper shaped like a pair of rabbit's ears*).

The menacing supernatural!

Think 'the supernatural' and many immediately think 'scary'. Indeed, while there are educators, parents/carers, and political and religious institutions who consider supernatural stories disturbing or harmful to children (see Dawkins in Knapton, 2014), Taylor (2010: iii) asserts that '[c]hildren's fascination with monsters is a normal part of childhood development'. Support child authors in considering the conflict that 'mysterious force[s] or being[s], representing things beyond rational scientific explanation' (Misra and R, 2012) can provide for their emerging written stories!

Early Years Foundation Stage

*   Introduce child authors to *Casper the Friendly Ghost* through video clips on *YouTube* (film or cartoon-based). Get them to think of things that Casper could do to them when he is having 'a bad day' e.g. *squirts toothpaste at them, trips them up* or *keeps turning the TV channel over*. Encourage them to mark make/write an emerging story about one of these incidents, considering how they stop this happening e.g. *send Casper to bed? Time out, perhaps? Talk to him sternly?*
*   Read *Aliens Love Underpants* (Freedman and Cort, 2007). Get child authors to imagine that they find an alien under their bed who has a passion for wearing a *different* item of clothing: *Socks? Hats? Gloves? Shoes? 'How could you get these back from off the alien – ask them politely? Scare them? Chase after them?'* Support them in mark making/writing an emerging story about one of their creative 'return' ideas.

Key stage 1

*   Give child authors some plastercine/moulding clay to create a 3D model of a monster. Get them to imagine that they open something at school – *a door/cupboard/box/drawer* – and find the monster there. *'It screams and so do you – ARGHHHHHHHH!'* Suggest that child authors write a short story about the problems the monster causes for them during the school day and why they eventually come to like it. *Does it help them to pass a spelling test, make new friends* or *get the better of the class bully?*
*   Chen (2014) suggests that 'supernatural wonder is derived from either a magical person (a fairy godmother, a wicked witch), a magical object (a wondrous beanstalk, a talking mirror...) or an enchantment (a miraculous sleep that lasts until love's first kiss)'. Get child authors to create their own supernatural wonder – *a mystical uncle, a meeting compass* or a *singing shoe* – weaving it into a stimulating story of conflict that causes 'the wonder' to be more of a hindrance for the protagonist rather than being of benefit e.g. *the shoes never stop singing!*

Gold star!

Noodlehead tales are described as 'light-hearted tales about silly people doing silly things' (Chen, 2014). Visit http://tinyurl.com/ckbfmvf, encouraging child authors to mark make/write emerging stories about crazy characters drinking tar, trying to walk on the ceiling or licking doors and humming! Add to the purposeful silliness by deliberately 'relaxing' spelling, grammar and punctuation conventions as the emerging story is mark made/written. *Perhaps child authors could try and write their story using their non-dominant hand?!*

Story writing 'pick and mix' 4

Here is a fourth collection of stimulating story writing ideas to engage child authors and enrich professional practices. As explained in 'Story writing "pick and mix" 1' (see p. 23) this assortment of ideas is not attributed to a particular age phase but is offered more as a selection of suggestions for professionals to choose from and adapt in response to the mark making/writing needs of their learners – *put an 'X' by any that you think you might try out!*

X
↓

	Story scenes: Offer child authors creative resources such as Fuzzy Felt, loom bands, cut-/silhouettes or mosaic sets to create a picture depicting a key object or scene in an emerging story. Invite child authors to regularly refer to this as they mark make/write their associated story to capture the important detail of the tale about (for example) a grumpy granny, a bottomless well or a school club.
	Story skipping rope: Build collaborative stories by hanging images/individual alphabet letters/(key) words/phrases/sentences/drawings/objects on an outstretched rope with bulldog clips to create sentences, sequence story events or create 'visual stories' in a story map style.
	Story signs: Visit http://tinyurl.com/opfm4l7, downloading relevant free *Makaton* resources. Support child authors in learning different signs, getting them to use one of these as the inspiration for some emerging story mark making/writing e.g. The magic *cake*, My *happy* dolly or Funny *hair* day.
	Story spray: Offer child authors empty/safe items which have a 'pump-action' device e.g. *perfume bottles, sun cream dispensers* and *deodorant cans*. Generate verbal ideas about unusual things which could come out of the containers when sprayed e.g. *music,* the *'flash'* of a camera, glitter or a magical scroll. Integrate this into a short story about a character who comes across a special spray at the supermarket and turns into a new character e.g. *Cream Man, Lavender Girl, Rosey Lady* or *Pongo the dog*. 'What do they get up to in their new identity?'
	Story chair: Place a chair in the middle of the carpet/room. Invite child authors to sit on the floor around it, taking it in turns to come and sit on the chair and initiate/continue an emerging verbal story. Suggest that listeners keep a simple 'log' (through drawings/words) of the story told on whiteboards, using this to mark make/write their own embellished retelling of the collaborative tale.
	Story suckers: 'Oh no! They're here! The Story Suckers! They sucking all the stories out of the libraries/bookshops – you've got to stop them! Quick!' Get child authors to write a race-against-time short story in which they help to save the world from being story-less by stopping the Story Sucker aliens from 'feeding' off tales from across the globe using their 'secret story saving weapon' (*whatever could it be?*).

Chapter 5

Resolving the problem/s!

Forgive and forget!

Research by Jose and Brewer (1983: 20) found that the 'liking of [a] story's outcome was determined by resolution of...a positive ending for young children and by the just world ending for older children'. One ending that can resolve the conflict in some stories is to 'forgive and forget'. There are many stories found in the Bible associated with the theme of forgiveness (see http://tinyurl.com/pjunfd9) – consider using these as a starting point to help child authors understand forgiveness as a decision/process/response for use in their emerging story mark making/writing.

Early Years Foundation Stage

- Blow up some balloons, telling child authors that you are going to a party. Organise for a fellow professional to come along and admire the balloons, handling them roughly so that they 'accidently' burst – **POP!** Ask child authors to think about how you feel and whether you should forgive your colleague or not. Support them in mark making/writing an emerging story about other situations (real/imagined) where they should be encouraged to forgive and forget about things others do to them and their possessions e.g. 'Jenny hid my dolly. I forgive her.' (Megan, 3.8 yrs, 'reading her writing'.)
- Read *We All Need Forgiveness* (Mayer, 2014). Get child authors to think about things they have done to others that might be considered unkind e.g. *not letting others play with them*, *pushing and teasing peers* or *being rude to Mummy*. Invite child authors to mark make/write an emerging 'reminder story' of what happened, giving their mark making/writing to the person(s) that they hurt – *will they/do they/have they forgiven them?*

Key stage 1

- Read *The Forgiveness Garden* (Thompson, 2012). Take child authors to visit a temporary Forgiveness Garden set up in the school grounds made by professionals and older children (think *fabrics*, *garlands*, *benches*, *shrubbery* and *plants*). Encourage child authors to recall something someone has done to them that they have been hurt by (be it physically or emotionally). Write this up as a short story on tree-shaped paper (taking care to use pseudonyms), 'planting' it around in the Forgiveness Garden in an effort to 'let go of the hurt'.

- Read *The Grudge Keeper* (Rockliff, 2014). Get child authors to write a short story about a story character who unfortunately has things of theirs broken or stolen, is lied to, or is hurt by others, presenting this on a nicely rolled up scroll (similar to those used by the residents of Bonnyripple) that can be given to the Grudge Keeper. *'Would it matter if the scrolls were thrown away, misplaced or a small flood destroyed them all, I wonder?'*

Gold star!

The Narrative Activity Pack (Calderdale & Huddersfield NHS Trust, 2012: 3) 'provide[s] practical ideas and resources for use at home and at school' in developing the narrative abilities of children. Download the pack from http://tinyurl.com/loq4rt3, considering the value of using activities advocated by the Trust to teach young child authors about *question words*, *sequencing* and *time*. Encourage them to apply this knowledge when they are mark making/writing their own emerging stories.

Seek help!

LifeCare (2011: 4) suggests that '[t]here may be times when, despite your best efforts, you may not be able to resolve a conflict on your own. If so, get help.' While professionals should actively encourage children to try and 'sort it out themselves' in an effort to build skills of independence, there will be occasions when they will need to request the assistance of peers, siblings and adults. This can be positively modelled through role play situations and their emerging story mark making/writing!

Early Years Foundation Stage

- Get child authors to mime different pets that they have at home – *can their peers guess what animal they are trying to act out?* Encourage them to talk about times when they have been in conflict with them – think *biting fingers*, *being noisy*, *jumping all over them* or *running away*. *'Who did you ask for help from to deal with these pesky pets?'* Get child authors to mark make/write an emerging story about those who helped them – think *siblings*, *parents/carers* and *grandparents*. *'How did you thank them for their help?'*
- Present child authors with a collection of clothing which have zips, press studs, Velcro and buttons on them. Challenge child authors to play a game where, with others, they have to put on and fasten three of the items the quickest – *who do they ask for help to be the winner?* Encourage them to mark make/write an emerging story about the clothes they put on, who helped them and if they won! Alternatively, challenge child authors to dress toy dolls that have a selection of different fastenings on their clothing.

Key stage 1

- Organise child authors into small groups and get them to collaboratively invent a pen that can do more than just write e.g. *fly, sew, play music, bark* or *dispense tape*. There is likely to be some conflict between individuals as they generate and decide on the best ideas. Make a note of who children seek support from to resolve this conflict e.g. *professionals, parent helpers* or *peers from other groups*. Use this experience as the basis of a written tale about the challenges of collective creativity!
- Read *Bully* (Seeger, 2015). Get child authors to think about occasions when they have been bullied, taking care *not* to identify the actual bully. *'What happened? Where did the bullying happen? How did it make you feel?'* Suggest that child authors write a fictional story about a bully, considering who the 'bullied' seeks help from to stop the bully from hurting them e.g. *professionals, parents/carers, siblings, peers, School Council members* or *class representatives*. *'How do they eventually manage to stop the bully?'*

Gold star!

Professionals can never have enough stories to tell and child authors can never read/be told enough stories! Fire their story mark making/writing imaginations with a wide range of stories (Hopwood-Stephens, 2013). Super online sources to extend professionals'/child authors' known bank of stories include:

Bed Time Stories – see http://tinyurl.com/ qhb3prp (apt for EYFS)	*Short Stories for Children* – see http://tinyurl.com/knf38pc (apt for KS1)

Using physical force!

One way to manage conflict is through physical force. This approach is understandably discouraged by settings and schools who actively promote the development of children's verbal conflict resolution skills (Coleman *et al.*, 2014); this Idea does not *in any way* challenge this quality practice. Within a 'safe' emerging story writing context, however, professionals might suggest that child authors use physical force as 'an option' to help them resolve certain difficulties that their story characters face, thus satisfying their primitive 'instinct[s]...to hit, shove, push, and yell' (Browning, n.d.: 2) – think *superheroes* and *pillow/foam fights!*

Early Years Foundation Stage

- *'Oh no! The monster from* Not Now, Bernard! *[McKee, 2012] has escaped from our big book in the outdoor play area and he is on his way into the nursery! Quick! How do we stop him from getting in?'* Get child authors to mark make/write an emerging story about different objects they would apply force to by pushing or pulling them in front of the doors of the setting to prevent the monster from entering and eating them all up!

- Show child authors how to make springs by wrapping thin wire around thick pens, pushing them into the feet of plastercine characters. Support them in mark making/writing an emerging story about how their characters are able to use spring force to make a quick escape from an approaching threat, such as *Deano the dreadful doggie* or *Marvin the metal munching robot* (BOING BOING!).

Key stage 1

- Get child authors to plan a little story of payback on the fictional 'Big Boy/Girl' who keeps deliberately pushing their lead story character over in the playground (for example). Suggest that they use tension force to trip up the bully with unseen string, rope, cable or wire while they are carrying something (books or their lunch), ensuring that the 'Big Boy/Girl' lands on something soft, such as grass, leaves or his friend! *Does this teach them a lesson?*
- Invite child authors to write a story about a magical eye-patch which, when worn, can cause the most incredible things to happen when the wearer winks with his exposed eye! Describe one of these amazing events in their story e.g. *a character is able to quickly reverse the force of gravity as a gigantic landslide approaches them* or *they can make sea waves 'wave' in the opposite direction*!

Gold star!

It is important that child authors develop their independence when engaging in emerging story mark making/writing activity (see Rumseya and Ballarda, 1985). While professionals can offer them support when needed, there are tangible independent story writing resources that can be purchased to supplement this support. Recommended sources include *Writing Prompt Cubes* (for ages 3+) and *Story Spinners* (for ages 5+), both available from *Amazon.co.uk*. Also see the *Early writing* (EYFS) and *Writing* resources (Primary) available from TTS Group.

Competitiveness!

An interesting way that story characters can resolve external conflict with others is through the use of competitions (see Bodenhafer, 1930). Opportunities for them to go head-to-head with 'the problem' (be it another person/animal/monster/machine/a force of nature/society/institution/abstract idea) allow child authors to build some exciting tension in their emerging story mark making/writing. *Who is going to win? Who will be defeated?* Think *competitive sports, reality TV shows* and *the Top 40 in the music industry*. The only way that readers will find out who is victorious is to keep on reading!

Early Years Foundation Stage

- Get a professional to 'work-in-role' (indicate this with a hat or a mask) as a slightly unpleasant character who thinks/verbalises how they are better than everyone else at physical activity. Set up little competitive activities in the outdoor play area to see if any child authors can throw/run/skip/hop/jump/catch/hit better than 'Mr/Little Miss Superior' – encourage them to mark make/write an emerging story about different activities where *they* outclass the professional – yeah!
- Challenge child authors to get dressed into their PE kits 'against the clock' – *can they beat their time from the previous week?* Support them in mark making/writing an emerging story about how they develop their changing skills over time e.g. *practicing 'their buttons' at home, seeking help from a friend* or *following a set sequence.*

Key stage I

- Introduce child authors to *Wordy William* (picture/puppet), a young character who *always* gets full marks in his spelling tests. Talk about how his superior abilities are resented by his classmates. *'How about challenging Wordy William to a different sort of word game – Boggle Bash!'* (see http://tinyurl.com/k7rop43). Get child authors to write a short story about the different words that competitors generate in class and the eventual winning score (who wins though)!
- Woledge (2013) claims that: '[C]ompetitive parents are splashing out increasing sums of cash on end of year gifts for teachers as they attempt to outdo each other at the school gates.' Encourage child authors to write a ridiculous story about the extravagant presents purchased for their teacher by fictional parents/carers. *'Whose gift is appreciated the most though by Miss Evans or Mr B? Why?'*

Gold star!

Visually support child authors' understanding of the various elements which make up a story (see Chapters 1–6 for ideas!) by presenting them on pieces of card shaped like lettuce leaves, tomatoes, cucumbers, radishes and other salad-type ingredients. 'Mix these' into a plastic bowl with a wooden spoon on the end of which is a pencil/pen for writing with – *what happens to the story if child authors forget to add the 'eggy' ending?* Alternatives could be elements presented on items that make up a stacked burger or the ingredients for layers of a cake.

Oh, I give in!

Peha (2003a: 17) asserts that: '[F]iction is all about how your character gets or does not get what he or she wants.' The song 'You Can't Always Get What You Want' by the Rolling Stones honestly reflects 'real life'; while it is disappointing, recognition and acceptance of this is all part of growing up to be a balanced human being. Professionals may question whether it is appropriate to advocate the notion of characters 'giving up' but they are reminded that it is just a story *option* and one which child authors *may* wish to use to bring some kind of resolution near the end of their emerging written story.

Early Years Foundation Stage

- Offer child authors different resources e.g. *kites, laces on cardboard shoes* or *jigsaws with many pieces* – items which they are likely to find tricky to engage with/complete. Empathise with their frustration, acknowledging that there are things that we all struggle to do and sometimes it is okay to give up. Support them in mark making/writing an emerging story about one of these activities in an effort to demonstrate traits such as being open and honest about one's abilities. *'Why not try again, soon?'*
- Read *Bea Gives Up Her Dummy* (Album, 2013). Get child authors to talk about things that they would find very hard to give up e.g. *sweets, their teddy bear, watching television* or *playing*. Invite them to mark make/write an emerging story about a real/imagined day when they try to give up a 'special thing' but do not succeed. Reassure them that they are not in any way a failure for not being able to give up these things. There are some things that we just *have* to do!

Key stage I

- Invite child authors to recall games they have played where they have given up trying to win e.g. *card games, running races* or *board games*. Get them to think about why they decided to do this and how it felt coming to that decision. Suggest that they write about one of these experiences as an anonymised story, acknowledging how it is difficult to compete against faster/stronger/lighter/more intelligent/well practised/more competitive children/adults. *'What do you always win at, though?'*
- Read *I Can Do It!* (Thomas, 2010). Invite child authors to write an accompanying 'sister' story book called *I Can't Do It!* in which they identify/describe things that they or their story characters have given up trying to do e.g. *read a difficult book, keep their bedroom tidy* or *teach their disobedient dog to sit* – think *Bart Simpson* and *Santa's Little Helper!*

Gold star!

Research by Graham and Perin (2007: 5) 'found strong evidence that pupils benefited from supporting each other. Such collaborative working involved a number of processes, including: reading, planning, drafting, revising, editing their compositions, [and] checking their final copies.' Ensure that there are opportunities for child authors you work with to engage with some or all of these processes when story mark making/writing, as appropriate and with the necessary support.

Avoiding one another!

Richardson (1995: 20) argues that '"avoidance" should, in some instances, be recognised as an active form of conflict resolution'. Parents/carers and professionals regularly encourage children to "avoid getting into trouble" in an effort to promote harmony with their peers and those around them; as such, avoidance can be offered as a 'powerful weapon' (p. 24) for child authors to utilise when attempting to resolve the conflict present in some of their emerging written stories.

Early Years Foundation Stage

• Get child authors to recollect an occasion when they have been in conflict with one of their peers in the setting over the ownership of toys or materials. *'How did that make you feel? How did you react?'* Model to child authors how to avoid getting into conflict with others by either ignoring their peers or walking away from the situation. Encourage them to mark make/write about this as an emerging 'reminder' story.

• Support child authors in talking about times when peers have tried to force others to play 'their way' or have wanted to be first in line – think *Me First!* (Lester, 1992). Get them to mark make/write an emerging story about how they can avoid these kinds of situations by calmly moving to another activity, turning their back on their peer or changing physical locations e.g. going from the indoor to the outdoor area.

Key stage I

• Nominate individuals to be a *Conflict Catcher*, taking digital images during playtime when children are in conflict with others. Show these images on the IWB in class by blurring out the children's faces, encouraging child authors to use the situation depicted as the stimulus for an avoidance story where story characters strategically ignore those who try to disrupt their gameplay with silly noises, 'body barriers', unpleasant name calling or 'flying fists'.

• There are times when fantasy play – think playing *pirates, soldiers, knights* and *police* – can turn boisterous and even violent. Support child authors in writing a short story in which their story characters' play 'escalates in intensity and tempers flare and frustration rises' (Isenberg and Jalongo, 2010): *'How do individuals avoid getting involved any further with this kind of behaviour?'*

Gold star!

The DfES (2001) produced some wonderful teaching materials to support professionals in delivering the *National Literacy Strategy* (NLS). While the strategy is now defunct, professionals are encouraged to download the PDF at http://tinyurl.com/n6djpzu, paying particular attention to pp. 1–7 in an effort to 'lift'/adapt quick-fire ideas, strategies and tips to improve/enrich the learning and teaching of emerging story writing in their settings/classrooms. An alternative PDF can be found at http://tinyurl.com/pjqorsy.

Let's reach a compromise!

Creffield (n.d.) argues that 'sometimes the only way to resolve a conflict is to compromise'. This can be problematic, not only for story characters but also for the child authors who mark make/write about them – professionals/children only have to read *The Day No One Played Together* (Helsley, 2011) to recognise the difficulties of reaching an agreement as a result of 'sides' making concessions. In an effort to help child authors develop the art of 'find[ing] ways of getting what they want without angering those around them' (Cunha, 2013), promote the use of compromise as one of their emerging story resolutions.

Early Years Foundation Stage

- When child authors argue over a toy in the setting use this as an opportunity to develop their understanding of compromise (see http://tinyurl.com/pcvqrz3). Talk about the idea of playing with it together or one person having it for a set period of time (via a large sand-timer perhaps?) and then passing it to the other. Mark make/write an emerging story about one of these solutions (or others) to the problem, displaying these for others to read, enjoy and learn from.
- Stereotypical perceptions of young children suggest that *they* want what *they* want when *they* want it. Role model this kind of behaviour during a circle time meeting, getting child authors to see how silly/rude/immature/unreasonable/demanding you can be. Get child authors to mark make/write an emerging story about someone who would be embarrassed to see this kind of behaviour in members of their immediate family e.g. *wider family members, themselves* or *peers* in an effort to help them understand how everyone needs to compromise, irrespective of their age.

Key stage 1

- Read *Crayon* (Rickerty, 2014). *'Have you ever squabbled with others about wanting to use particular crayons when drawing pictures?'* Rather than use the *'Let him use the red crayon and then you [use it]'* strategy, talk about the following suggestions: *'He uses the red and you can use the brown, then you can switch'* or *'Let's watch him use the red crayon to learn what you might do when he gives you the crayon'* (see Forman, 2013). Get child authors to incorporate these strategies into a short compromise story involving the spiders from *Crayon* and their weaving of webs or feasting on flies.
- North (2015) advocates the idea of children asking if they 'may have a compromise'. Visit http://tinyurl.com/kw8fd95 to see how the strategy works, discussing and modelling it during PHSCE learning opportunities. Get child authors to use it in a written story where different characters have to compromise over situations that involve either food (*when to eat*), money (*how much to spend*), television programmes (*what to watch*) or holiday activities (*what to do and when to do them*).

Gold star!

There are times when professionals need access to a wealth of *additional* practical resources/strategies/ideas that they can pick and choose from (see 'Story writing "pick and mix" 1–10' at the end of each chapter!). Visit http://tinyurl.com/c4ta6w, selecting from the *102 Resources for Fiction Writing* that can be adapted and incorporated into your practice in response to the 'narrative needs' of the child authors you have the good fortune of working with.

Let's talk it out!

Evans (2011: 3) advocates professionals supporting children in 'talking through a problem and agreeing on a solution' to effectively deal with conflict that they experience with others. By engaging in this important activity child authors can use this as a valuable strategy to resolve the problems that characters have in their emerging written stories; this also gives many of them the opportunity to develop and hone their abilities of devising and recording 'spoken words' (dialogue) as part of their storytelling/mark making/writing (Strauss, 2010: 94).

Early Years Foundation Stage

• Get child authors to think about situations when they have been in conflict with one of their peers e.g. *unwilling to share resources*, *unable to take turns* or *being physically hurt*. Encourage them to role play one of these scenarios with professionals, considering how they could use hand signals (*Stop!*) or talk 'to give a justification, reason, alternative proposal, or to refer to rules' (Thornberg, 2006: 8). Offer them an opportunity to record this scenario on paper as a little emerging story with support and encouragement.

• Mathieson (2005: 34) advocates the use of puppets to help 'children explore with you the different ways a particular conversation could develop'. Offer child author puppets (made in the setting/purchased), encouraging them to 'play out' a conversation where one puppet has verbally upset the other by calling them a nasty name. Get them to mark make/write an emerging story about how saying 'Sorry' and giving each other a hug can usually ease the tension between them (see *I'm Sorry* by McBratney (2001) for inspiration).

Key stage 1

• KidsHealth in the Classroom (2006: 2) asserts that '[f]airy tales are loaded with conflict'. Support child authors in using 'working-in-role' techniques such as *paired improvisation* or *flash forwards* (see http://tinyurl.com/kmgeh85, p. 3) when taking on 'characters in conflict' e.g. 'Goldilocks breaking into the bears' house [or] Cinderella being treated unfairly by her stepmother' (KidsHealth in the Classroom, 2006: 2). Write a simple story about how they (the characters) work together by talking to each other to resolve their conflict.

- Cureton *et al.* (in Kreidler and Whittall, 1999) propose the 'Talk It Out Together' method of solving conflicts. Download the PDF at http://tinyurl.com/pe34uxz, teaching child authors to use the method in their daily efforts to deal with issues of conflict. Encourage them to exemplify this method as part of a written story of conflict between siblings (sibling rivalry) as a result of competitiveness, issues of attention seeking or jealousy.

Gold star!

It is recognised that there are many genres of stories for child authors to read and write (see Haloin *et al.*, 2005). As contemporary twenty-first-century authors and professionals, broaden child authors' appreciation of unusual story genres (seek suitable examples from http://tinyurl.com/78nv97t) by telling them invented unusual stories and encouraging them to mark make/write unusual emerging stories! Personal favourites include *Pop-Up Picture Books* (apt for EYFS) and *Undersea* (apt for KS1).

Problems seeking solutions!

Cairney (2009) identifies problem solving as one of the key themes in children's literature due to the fact that 'many children love to solve problems'. He argues that there are many forms of problem solving which authors can capitalise on, and this Idea explores some of those proposed that child authors could use in their own emerging story mark making/writing to ensure their tale has a much needed 'complication' (Cleaver, 2006: 18) to stop it from 'sagging in the middle'.

Early Years Foundation Stage

- Get child authors to think of times when they have had an argument with one of their peers. Get them to role play this with the use of masks, hats or dressing-up clothes. Mark make/write about how they found a solution to the argument e.g. *saying sorry to one another*, '*kiss and make up*', *talking it through* or *keeping their distance from one another for a period of time*. Display these solutions in the setting as an emerging story 'for reference' of what children can do when they find themselves in conflict with a peer.
- Encourage child authors to identify different devices in the setting that have not worked for them e.g. *computers, digital cameras, Bee-Bots, CD players, torches* or *microphones*. '*What did you do about it? Ask someone for help? Experiment (play) with it? Get some new batteries? Pretend that it was working?*' Invite child authors to mark make/write an emerging story about one way they eventually solved their problem with ICT resources.

Key stage 1

- Read *The Lighthouse Keeper's Lunch* (Armitage and Armitage, 2007). Get child authors to discuss and draw inventive ways to address the real-life problem of the greedy seagulls e.g. *create a papier-mâché seagull to 'fly' the lunch in, electrify the basket with a small battery charge* or *fire the lunch towards the lighthouse via a jet-propelled catapult*. Invite child authors to write their creative idea as part of a fictional story for the *Lighthouse Keeper* (professional-in-role) to evaluate in terms of its creativity and ingenuity.
- Talk to child authors about an imaginary maths test, which a story character takes and fails – show them a mock answer sheet with red crosses all over the page (F)! *'What could the character do to make sure they pass the test the next time they take it?'* Get child authors to reflect on strategies they use in their own maths lessons/numeracy sessions to achieve success e.g. *use counters, practise, seek help, work with others, use a calculator, work it out on paper* or *double check their answers*. Weave these different strategies in a helpful story for the story character (and readers) to learn from.

Gold star!

StoryJumper is a wonderful website which allows child authors to create their own story books with support that can be published online and as an actual book. Visit the site (see http://tinyurl.com/yek8v78), paying particular attention to the *StoryStarter – Tell a story in 7 steps* webpage (http://tinyurl.com/oxnv2nf) which offers a wealth of smashing story ideas for adoption and adaption to supplement those proposed by both child authors and professionals.

Story writing 'pick and mix' 5

Here is a fifth collection of stimulating story writing ideas to engage child authors and enrich professional practices. As explained in 'Story writing "pick and mix" 1' (see p. 23) this assortment of ideas is not attributed to a particular age phase but is offered more as a selection of suggestions for professionals to choose from and adapt in response to the mark making/writing needs of their learners – *put an 'X' by any that you think you might try out!*

X
↓

Story experiences: Malindine (2012: 8) asserts that child authors should '[t]ry to write a story that comes from your own experience'. Encourage child authors to source potential lived occurrences (be they amusing, sad, disastrous or outrageous) for their emerging story with reference to photographs, videos or conversations with parents / carers.
Story sacks: Story sacks are described by the National Literacy Trust (n.d.b: 1) as 'a large cloth bag containing a favourite children's book with supporting materials to stimulate language activities and make reading a memorable and enjoyable experience' (see http:// tinyurl.com/jwmpb8l for further details). Invite child authors to collaborate together to create a *new* story book for a *new* story sack along with all of the supporting materials such as puppets, masks and matching-pairs card games relating to the story!
Story bonanza: Encourage child authors to mark make / write emerging stories for a *Story Bonanza* stall at the setting's / school's Christmas / Summer fête, selling tales that have been written for potential buyers who attend the event e.g. *parents / carers, friends* and *siblings.*
Story sensation: Suggest that child authors mark make / write an emerging story which they believe will be the next 'literary sensation' in story writing (think *Meg and Mog; The Jolly Postman*). Offer these to local publishers / authors to critique (where possible), identifying select stories which they feel should be included on the setting's / school's website. Professionals could also possibly involve local book sellers in this along with local public libraries as a possible display publicity opportunity. Links could also be made to World Book Day or Children's Book Week celebrations.
Story Telling into Writing: Corbett (2006: 1) claims that 'the best writers in a class are always avid readers', an assertion well supported by personal observations of working with child authors in various settings / schools. Dip into the PDF (see http://tinyurl.com/ lu9aodv), considering the value of utilising advocated practices by the brilliant literacy educationalist.
Funny story: Amusing things happen to people all the time. Get child authors to think about amusing things that have happened to them – *wearing odd socks to the setting / school, getting locked in the toilet* or *falling over a pile of dirty washing at home* – mark making / writing these up as an emerging story with a smile on their face!
Story writing book: In collaboration with colleagues discuss some of the content of *Schaum's Quick Guide to Writing Great Short Stories* (Lucke, 1999 – see http://tinyurl.com/n34ps8f) at a team / staff meeting, considering its value in developing planning, improving provision, and enriching learning and teaching practices in the setting / classroom / school.

Chapter 6

All's well that ends well!

Take my advice!

Peha (2003b: 91) argues that while there are not many types of story endings, the first of the 16 that he identifies is '[e]nding with some advice'. He asserts that 'it makes for a good ending...tell[ing] other humans what we think they should do' (p. 91). In an effort to thus help readers learn from the experiences of story characters, encourage child authors to end their emerging stories with some supportive recommendations; after all, 'endings are about change' (Rinzler, 2011) and there is no way better to achieve this than by (potentially) changing the life of those who actually read the story!

Early Years Foundation Stage

- Encourage child authors to wear items from a box of mixed seasonal dressing-up clothes. Support them in thinking about what would happen if they wore the wrong clothes when it is sunny/windy/rainy/snowy. Invite them to mark make/write an emerging story which advises others about suitable attire for different weather conditions e.g. 'Wear gloves when it snows' (story dictation, Jackson, 3.6 yrs).
- Wiseman (2014: 5–6) reports that 'the vast majority of children arrive at school overtired'. Get child authors to talk about different times they have been tired and how they reacted to this e.g. *they were teary, angry, moody, quiet* or *fed up*. Suggest that child authors mark make/write an emerging story about why we should all get more sleep – '*What kind of exciting things can you do when you have had a good night's sleep?*' – and how this can be achieved e.g. *having a bedtime bear, drinking warm milk* or *taking a nice warm bath before bed*.

Key stage 1

- Introduce child authors to a toy animal who dreams of being able to fly. Encourage them to generate a list of different ways this could be achieved e.g. *booster pack, balloons, magic powder* or *a gigantic spring*. Get child authors to write a short story in which the anthropomorphised animal endures a failed attempt (but is not hurt), ending the story with some gentle advice about how it is safer to fly in aeroplanes, helicopters and jets with helmets and seatbelts.

- Show child authors a *children's* lottery ticket (see http://tinyurl.com/nw25g44). Get them to imagine that they have won the jackpot. *'How much did you win? What do you intend to spend the money on?'* But wait! *'Oh no! You've only gone and misplaced the ticket – what are you going to do?'* Invite them to write a 'searching story', ending the tale with some practical advice about the importance of looking after important papers and documents and how to achieve this e.g. *using safes, folders, labelled drawers* and *box files.*

Gold star!

One way that young child authors can learn to 'write well' is through the advice given by literary agents (Sambuchino, 2013). Visit http://tinyurl.com/ccrbfjf, sharing age-appropriate snippets of feedback or adapted advice to help child authors improve aspects of their story mark making/writing. Personal favourites include avoiding 'endless "laundry list" character descriptions' and 'feeling cheated [by] the protagonist waking up'. Alternatively, see http://tinyurl.com/lwmq2v4 or http://tinyurl.com/kfjbttf for information and ideas.

Lessons learned!

All writing has a purpose, be it to inform, educate, entertain or persuade. When mark making/writing emerging stories Johns (2004) guards against writers simply 'telling the story of what happened. Readers usually want to know what [was] learned' *as a result* of what occurred. Professionals will recognise that there are many fables and fairy tales which end with a moral or a 'lesson learned'; *The Boy Who Cried Wolf* and *Cinderella* serve as two classic examples. Help child authors to strengthen their emerging story endings by teaching their characters (and readers) some valuable life lessons!

Early Years Foundation Stage

- Get child authors to talk about suitable or appropriate adverse things that have recently happened to them e.g. *catching a cold, getting paint on their clothes* or *falling over.* Support them in mark making/writing a 'What-I've-Learned' emerging story based on their lived experiences e.g. 'Look where you're running!' (Dylan, 3.7 yrs, reading aloud his mark making.)
- Read *Share and Take Turns* (Meiners, 2003). Introduce child authors to *It's Mine Mouse* and *Me First Frog* (in the form of puppets or soft toys), emphasising their poor social skills. Help child authors to mark make/write an emerging story to educate one of these characters in ways to effectively share or take turns e.g. *setting time limits for 'Show and Tell', dividing objects into equal piles* or *playing simple board games together.*

Key stage 1

- There are occasions when school toys get damaged or broken. Encourage child authors to write a short story about what happens to story characters who *deliberately* break toys e.g. *they have to have 'Time Out', pay for them to be repaired or replaced* or *write a letter of apology to the toy.* Watch http://tinyurl.com/nos7efr as a humorous warning of what can happen!
- 'It starts with stories and pretending; the ability to believe' (Johnson, 2014). Challenge child authors to imagine that nothing is impossible. *'What would you like to happen to your story character today? Will they become a sailor, turn into a pair of scissors, hibernate for three months, write a pop song or live their life for the day backwards* (night-time through to morning)*?'* Use the life lesson of believing that *anything* is possible to promote some truly creative story writing!

Gold star!

The brilliant *Toy Story* trilogy (Disney Pixar) serves as a wonderful stimulus for helping child authors to learn valuable 'lessons'. Indeed, the Oh My Disney (2013) blog *What We Learned From Toy Story* suggests that the toys have 'a lot of wisdom to impart, inspirational, practical, and otherwise'. See http://tinyurl.com/osw3apg for 20 'lessons' which child authors could use/adapt for the benefit of their own emerging story mark making/writing with support from professionals. Watch video clips from the different films to help child authors understand the 'lessons' through a 'seeing-is-believing' approach.

A time to reflect

Peha (2003b: 97) asserts that:

> Often, when we find ourselves at the end of something, we want to make a judgment about it. We look back over the entire experience and ask ourselves: Was it good? Was it bad? How did things turn out for me? What's the bottom line? And then we try to sum things up as best we can.

This succinctly describes what child authors can do, with support, if they wish to use a reflective ending to 'tie up' their emerging story. Brownhill (2014: 133) identifies a wealth of strategies to promote reflective thought, and a selection of these serve as the 'trigger' for some reflective emerging story endings.

Early Years Foundation Stage

- Invite child authors to bring in photographs of family members, pets or friends whom they have not seen for a long time or who have unfortunately passed away. Encourage them to talk about happy or amusing memories of these individuals/animals. Get them to mark make/write a reflective 'flash sentence' (an adaption of *flash fiction* – see Emery, 2012) which succinctly summarises how they feel about the time they had with their granny, hamster or former 'bestie'.

- Take child authors on an exploration of the local park or woods. Use this as an opportunity for them to recall times they have been there with their family/friends. *'What happened?'* Offer them clipboards and pencils to mark make/write an emerging story 'in situ', reflecting on the time Mummy fell into a puddle or Paddy the dog ran off after a rabbit. *'What did they learn from this experience – beware of hidden puddles? Hold tight onto Paddy's lead?'*

Key stage 1

- Read *The Jolly Postman* (Ahlberg and Ahlberg, 1999). Get child authors to undertake the 'Map Exercise' as described by Polka Theatre (n.d.: 6–7 – see http://tinyurl.com/mrc3dpg). Once complete, encourage them to reflect on the Jolly Postman's day in terms of the 'highs and the lows' of delivering the post to the different story characters. *'Which parts of the day did he enjoy/not enjoy? How do you know?'* Invite child authors to write a recall story on the back of a large envelope, concluding it by considering whether the Jolly Postman likes his job and whether he is looking forward to 'posting' tomorrow.
- Present child authors with a selection of baby objects for them to handle e.g. *booties, dummies, bibs, rattles, soft blankets, nappies* and *toys*. Get them to talk about what these items remind them of, be it personal or in relation to siblings or others. Encourage them to write a story which uses one of these baby objects as the 'driving force' of the tale e.g. *The Lost Dummy, The Noisy Rattle* or *The Broken Toy*, all of which end with some reflection as to whether the experience was positive or not.

Gold star!

There are some real gems on the internet to support professionals in stimulating the story mark making/writing of child authors they work with. Consider the value of the following PDFs to enrich and 'transform' story mark making/writing practices in your setting/classroom:

- http://tinyurl.com/bnpjksg
- http://tinyurl.com/m5nnmvo

- http://tinyurl.com/bnpjksg
- http://tinyurl.com/n489hb6

A not-so-happy ending!

It is common for children's stories to have a happy ending. However, many well-known stories do not actually have the typically Disney-fied 'contented conclusion' as many of us believe; in the original version of *The Little Mermaid* (Andersen, 2014), for example, the prince marries a different woman resulting in the title character throwing herself into the sea where her body dissolves into sea foam! Invite child authors to join the likes of the Brothers Grimm and engage in the 'lost art' of mark making/writing emerging stories that do not close on a happy note!

Early Years Foundation Stage

- Offer child authors a range of origami animals (visit http://tinyurl.com/dy2j6bd). Get them to select one, verbalising exciting antics that they could get up to together e.g. *playing hide and seek in the dark, taking part in a bit of home-grown karaoke* or *drinking fizzy pop to make them burp loudly!* Support them in mark making/writing an emerging story based on one of these antics after they find *The Hole-Punch Monster* has unfortunately 'chewed' their chosen animal to bits (remind them that it is just pretend!).

- Suggest child authors draw images/mark make/write an emerging story about an occasion when they lost at something e.g. *a running race, eating their dinner the slowest* or *the cupcake decorating/painting competition*. As they engage with their mark making/written work encourage them to talk how it felt when they did not win. '*Were you sad? A little down? Teary? Unhappy? Did you get over it in the end – did a hug from Mummy help?*'

Key stage 1

- Read *Goodnight Mog* (Kerr, 2003). Support child authors in sensitively talking about pets or family members who have unfortunately passed away e.g. *grandparents or aunties/uncles*. Encourage them to write a short story in which they find out that a well-known fictional character has fallen into an 'eternal sleep'. *What is their reaction to this news? How do they try and remember them?*

- Stimulate child authors' imaginations by playing the latest chart music on the radio in the classroom. Get them to imagine that as a class they are entered by their teacher into a national *Glee*-style competition and subsequently win! The prize is a recording contract but success is short-lived for them when their first single does not make the Top 40/Billboard 100. Support them in retelling this in their own disappointed words. '*Does it matter that they are not a success? Do they still have each other as friends?*'

Gold star!

The inspiration for this idea came from viewing Saunders *et al.*'s (2009: 138) research 'onion'. Support child authors in considering the 5W[1]H cues (Jasper, 2006) – *Who? Where? What? When? Why? How?* – at the planning stage of their emerging story mark making/writing by labelling up and jotting down ideas in concentric circles with support. Alternatively, use this diagram layout as a visual prompt/display idea for helping child authors to consider/remember the different story elements (refer to http://tinyurl.com/d6soj4r).

A time to remember

It is said that 'death comes to us all', irrespective of race, creed or sex. When 'the end' does come many people spend time thinking about loved ones who have passed away which can comfort them. Stories such as *Gentle Willow* (Mills, 2003) and *Michael*

Rosen's Sad Book (Rosen, 2004) help readers (and child authors themselves) to recognise and positively address feelings of disbelief, anger and sadness, along with love and compassion. Encourage child authors to use the notion of 'looking back' as a poignant way to bring an emerging written story to a conclusion following a story character's passing.

Early Years Foundation Stage

*   Get child authors to sensitively talk about pets they have had that have died. Invite them to reminisce about a time when their pet did something which made them smile or laugh. Suggest that they mark make/write about this occasion as an emerging recollection story, illustrating their story to capture the picture they have in their mind of the incident.
*   Invite child authors to bring in photographs from home of a family member who has passed away. Get them to sensitively talk about this person, reflecting on who they were and what child authors liked about them. Get them to mark make/write an emerging story of a memorable time with them as a touching way to remember them, presenting their mark making/writing on a large cardboard tag that is attached to a helium-filled balloon which is released into the open sky.

Key stage I

*   Talk to child authors about how some people plant trees as a way of remembering people. Get child authors to plant some flowering seeds as a way of remembering friends who have either moved schools or away from the local area. Invite them to write an unforgettable story which involves the child author and their special friend – *can they write it in a way that is unforgettable for the reader e.g. on the outline of a large tree or on the outside of a 3D paper-folded flower?*
*   Show child authors a blank picture frame. Get them to imagine someone or something that has passed away. *'What can you see in the picture frame? What do they look like? What features make them vivid in your mind?'* Get child authors to focus on these features, using these as the inspiration for an 'Inspired by...' story e.g. Tabby's *ginger hair* might inspire a story about a stick of orange candy floss which tries to escape from being eaten or Grandad's *blue eyes* might inspire a story about a make-up model's nightmare day in front of the camera!

Gold star!

It is strongly believed, from a personal perspective, that research should inform professional practice. With this in mind, professionals are encouraged to actively read and discuss the content of one of the research papers overleaf, considering the implications (if any) for a possible mini-action research project into the learning and teaching of emerging story mark making/writing in your setting/classroom:

Research title	Author(s) and date	Weblink
Learning to read and write: A longitudinal study of 54 children from first through fourth grades	Juel (1988)	http://tinyurl.com/oz28tcy
Creativity, uncertainty and discomfort: Teachers as writers	Cremin (2006)	http://tinyurl.com/ozqq3mv
Storytelling and story writing: 'Using a different kind of pencil'	Campbell and Hlusek (2009)	http://tinyurl.com/l5aa8hf

Ending with a question?!

It is no secret that readers can feel let down by the ending of a story if they do not consider it to be 'good'; as such, Peha (2003b: 90) recognises story endings as being 'the hardest things to write'. One way to make story endings memorable for all the right reasons is through the use of a question, be it rhetorical (Peat, 2010) or one that actually does require an answer! Professionals can support child authors by helping them to develop an understanding of different question types and how these can be used to stimulate the final line of their emerging tale!

Early Years Foundation Stage

- Invite child authors to contribute a page to a collaborative group/setting story called *The Colour Hunt!* by locating an object in the setting which is of a particular colour, mark making/writing about this on a separate piece of paper e.g. 'I found green on the door' (story dictation, Sanjeet, 3.4 yrs). Once the book has been collated and read, offer the question *Which is your favourite colour and why?* at the end of the book to generate some verbal discussion when it is read.
- *Where's Spot?* (Hill, 2009) uses a simple question to engage young readers. Support child authors in creating the final scene for an adapted '*Where's _____ now?*' story, hiding themselves or another animal under one of a number of paper/card/fabric flaps. Offer the question *Where's _____ now?* in an effort to stimulate exclamations between the reader and the book: '*He is not unbr the mat*' (Alan, 4.10 yrs, independent writing).

Key stage 1

- Orally tell child authors a simple story of a boy who dreams that he has a ship made of clouds that he sails through the sky at night to exciting locations. Suggest that they write a story about their own 'dreamy' sailing ship. '*Where do you go in it? Who do you meet? What happens there?*' At the end of the story, when they wake from their dream, offer the questions '*I wonder where I will sail to tonight? What do you think?*' to provoke some thought in those reading or marking the story!

- Invite child authors to write a story about a character who overzealously sends out a large number of birthday invitations and has to cope with an influx of individuals to their party! Offer the question *'How many came to the party in the end?'* to promote active counting, keeping in mind Whitin and Whitin's (2004: 4) calling for 'ethnic, gender, and cultural inclusiveness' in the text and illustrations that child authors provide.

Gold star!

Visit http://tinyurl.com/mxetyc for images of *17 Larger Than Life Giant Objects*! Get child authors to select one of these objects, considering what happened the day the object suddenly appeared in their setting/school. Enrich their emerging written tales by 'building up' the object's presence e.g. *'What if it could talk or move?'* Alternatively, have child authors come into the setting/class to find a giant biscuit/Ferrero Rocher/My Purple Bar/Toblerone/Gummi Worm. *'Who put it there? Where did it come from? Do you think they want it back?'*

A twist-in-the-tale ending!

Singleton and Conrad (2000: 229) define a plot twist as 'a radical change in the expected direction or outcome of the plot of a novel, film, television series, comic, video game, or other work of narrative'. Many readers like to be surprised by what they read and Jeffrey Archer is personally considered to be a master of 'the surprise/shock ending' (see Archer, 2014). While professionals would rightly argue that Archer's stories are not suitable for child authors, the 'mechanics' that he and other established authors use to 'twist the tale' can be embraced by child authors to bring an element of the unexpected to the finale of their own emerging stories!

Early Years Foundation Stage

- Offer select child authors a collection of dressing-up clothes – *hats, costumes, wigs, masks* and *glasses* – that can be combined together to create a new character. Invite other child authors to discover (guess) who is 'inside the character' by the way that they move, talk and behave. Draw/mark make/write an emerging story about what gives the character away e.g. 'Molly likes pink too!' (story dictation, Harry, 4.0 yrs).
- Show child authors a plate of delicious cupcakes (real/toy). Count them out, acting surprised when you find one of them is missing. *Where has it gone? Who has taken it?* Support child authors in behaving like detectives, identifying possible culprits and reasoning for the disappearance of the cupcake e.g. *Daddy ate it because he had a rumbling tummy*; *Wilf the dog took it because he liked the sweet smell*; *Marcy the magpie stole it because of its gold and silvery icing*. Suggest that they mark make/write their ideas up as an emerging 'mini-story'. *Who did take the cupcake in the end – was it you?!*

Key stage I

- Encourage child authors to write a short adventure story about two friends, one brave (e.g. a dog) and the other timid (e.g. a kitten). *'Where do they go on their adventure? What do they see? What problem do they encounter? A river/lion/ monster/an electric fence?'* Suggest that they surprise the reader by making the timid friend 'the brave one' as the dog actually turns out to be a 'scaredy-cat' when faced with danger!
- Talk to child authors about *Evil Eric*, an unpleasant boy you 'know' who likes to design and make cardboard devices to capture small animals in such as birds, mice and rabbits. Talk about how horrid these traps are: *'How do you think an animal feels if/when they get caught in one of these devices?'* Get child authors to write a descriptive story in which 'poetic justice' occurs with the help of characters such as *Conservation Charlie, Caring Cuthbert* or *Kind Kim/Katie* e.g. *the trap does not work, an animal easily escapes the trap* or Evil Eric *gets caught in the trap!*

Gold star!

An impressive professional resource is Shaw's (2008) *1001 Brilliant Writing Ideas*. Consider visiting http://tinyurl.com/myxn5y2 for a downloadable PDF of the book, complementing the immense wealth of ideas offered with those in this book and its sister volume (*Stimulating Story Writing! Inspiring children aged 7–11* – see Brownhill, 2016).

Cliffhanger!

Bowkett (2010: 49) describes cliffhangers as a 'narrative device [which] ends the scene or chapter at a dramatic moment, leaving the reader wanting more'. They can, of course, be used to *end* a story although there are many who would argue that this leaves the reader (and possibly the author) 'unsatisfied'. Nevertheless, child authors of all ages should be encouraged to mark make/write with the intention of making their readers 'want more' – *the question is whether they actually succeed!*

Early Years Foundation Stage

- Organise it for child authors to bring in their favourite teddy bear from home. Get them to think of imaginary situations where their teddy would be in danger in the setting e.g. *dangling off the top of the climbing frame, stepping in front of an oncoming tricycle* or *falling head first into the toilet bowl*! Talk to child authors about 'secret stories' where only the writer knows the ending. Get them to mark make/write an emerging story about their dangerous scenario, displaying these for peers to 'guess what happens at the end'.
- Read a brand new story book to child authors that they have not seen before, stopping at a 'critical point' for the main character in the tale (a *mid-cliffhanger* in the telling of the tale!). Get child authors to orally discuss what they think is

going to happen next, recording their story ideas on paper with marks/writing. Return to the book and complete the reading – *how does their story, post-mid-cliffhanger, compare? Were their ideas better than the one that was published?*

Key stage 1

- Bell (2004) suggests there are nine different types of cliffhangers, examples of which include *impending disaster, mysterious dialogue* and *surprise.* Support child authors in thinking about dangerous situations (*being strapped to a firework*), whispered words spoken by an imaginary character ('*Is anyone home?*') or events that startle (*chocolate money growing out of the ground*) that they can use to end a 'story short' with. Inspire reluctant writers with *humorous* cliffhangers e.g. *falling into a bowl of custard, it begins to rain tomato ketchup* or *a character steps out of the computer game that is being played!*
- As Halloween approaches invite child authors to write a spooky-themed story involving ghosts, vampires, monsters and/or skeletons set in a haunted location e.g. *a graveyard, an old house* or *a secret cellar.* Support them in ending the story with a 'creepy' cliffhanger e.g. *The coffin lid slowly creaked opened…; The front door slammed shut – BANG!; It all suddenly went very, very **dark!***

Gold star!

Let child authors into *your* story writing world by sharing examples of *your* story writing with them (notional/actual), giving them opportunities to learn from your efforts, be they positive or not so positive. *Can they help you to make your story better? **Of course they can!*** If child authors see professionals as living authors they are more likely to aspire to be an author themselves (see Grainger, 2005; Ings, 2009)!

A possible sequel?

How many times have you asked yourself '*I wonder what happens next?*' or '*Is there another one?*' after reading a good book? Many published authors satisfy their readers' curiosity/desire by writing sequels which typically form part of a series; this is particularly evident in children's literature – think *The Mr. Men/Little Miss* books and *Thomas the Tank Engine.* Develop child authors' emerging story mark making/writing abilities by 'continuing the story' which is what a 'follow up' is all about!

Early Years Foundation Stage

- Get child authors to draw their favourite character from a picture story book series, drawing by the side of them something which has not appeared in any of the different stories that they have heard/seen/read before e.g. *a bus stop, a star fish, a doughnut* or *a shopping bag.* Mark make/write about the significance of this new item as an emerging story e.g. *Maisy's shopping bag* or *Splat the cat and the delicious doughnut!*

• Offer child authors a selection of picture books for them to sort them into those that belong to a series and those that are 'standalone'. Get child authors to think about 'the day after' different story characters have had their respective adventures that are recorded in a book: *'What do you think they do the next day?'* Encourage child authors to mark make/write an emerging story about unusual events such as them growing another arm, falling down the plughole or learning to walk on their head!

Key stage 1

• Film sequels usually have a number at the end of the title to indicate its chronological place in the series e.g. *Cars 2*; *Toy Story 3*. Get child authors to select a favourite story from the school's reading scheme(s), adding a '2' or a little subtitle (:_____) to the main title which serves as the inspiration for a new story based on a familiar tale e.g. *Silly Races 2*; *Looking after Gran: The Lost Teeth* (both adapted from the *Oxford Reading Tree* reading scheme).

• Challenge child authors to find story books in the school library which are based around events which happen once a year e.g. *a birthday party*, *the school fayre*, *Christmas* or *SATS!* Get child authors to select one story, using this as the basis (in terms of characters and setting) for an 'annual sequel', considering what happens a year on since the last incident!

Gold star!

Sipe (1993: 19) asserts that known stories can be renovated by writing 'parallel, deconstructed, or extended versions of the original tale, or the tale may be transformed through the illustrations'. Support child authors in understanding how published authors have achieved this by showing them printed examples from '[a]n annotated bibliography of transformations of traditional stories' (see pp. 25–26 of Sipe's article for a useful list), using these as a verbal/written model for their own story mark making/writing.

Story writing 'pick and mix' 6

Here is a sixth collection of stimulating story writing ideas to engage child authors and enrich professional practices. As explained in 'Story writing "pick and mix" 1' (see p. 23) this assortment of ideas is not attributed to a particular age phase but is offered more as a selection of suggestions for professionals to choose from and adapt in response to the mark making/writing needs of their learners – *put an 'X' by any that you think you might try out!*

X
↓

Story wheel: Engage child authors at the planning stage of their emerging story writing with a story wheel. Visit http://tinyurl.com/njkke37, adapting the instructions to allow child authors to use the individual wheel wedges to consider different story elements (character, setting, plot etc.) using illustrations and marks/text. Alternatively, get child authors to create a story wheel in which each stage of their emerging story is written on sections of the wheel.

Stories and materials: Encourage child authors to present their emerging story mark making/writing in a diverse range of exciting materials e.g. *glitter, milk powder, sawdust shavings, coffee granules, spices, sugar* or *dry tea leaves.* Take digital images to capture the emerging story produced before it is erased or, alternatively, offer them glue and card/paper to capture a mirror record of the finished work by placing the card/paper face down on the material!

Selfie story: In response to the popularity of the 'selfie' (a self-portrait photograph taken with a hand-held digital camera or camera phone) suggest that child authors write an emerging story that involves *them* as the lead character, thus creating a 'selfie story'!

Story letter: Give each child author a coloured envelope, inside which can be found a folded piece of paper, be it lined, plain, coloured and/or shaped. Invite them to mark make/write an emerging story on the paper which can be then sent to the recipient of their choice by hand or by postal mail. As an extension idea, offer child authors the name of a story character/real person/famous person in the envelope, inviting child authors to mark make/write an emerging story for or involving this character/person.

Story deception: 'It is said that appearances are deceptive. How would you change your appearance with a disguise and what would you get up to when you are "incognito"?' Offer child authors the dressing-up box or computer art programs to help them alter their look (real/digital) and stimulate their 'slippery' emerging storytelling!

Story loss: Read an age-appropriate version of the biblical story of *Samson and Delilah.* Get child authors to identify other things that can be cut or trimmed from our bodies – *nails (finger/toe), beards, eyebrows, nose hair, ear hair* and *eyelashes* – and the effect this has on story characters in their own emerging story. 'What do they lose? Their confidence? Their ability to sleep? Their sense of time? Their ability to do magic tricks? Their balance? Does "their loss" come back in time?'

Part II

Stimulating emerging story writing provision and practice

Chapter 7

Inspired ideas!

Planning with ease!

There is a shared understanding in the story writing community that writing is 'a sequence of steps, with planning the organisation of the content [the plot] as one of these' (BBC, 2009: 3). The importance of story planning cannot be underestimated; for many child authors it can make the difference between them getting lost in a 'wealth of ideas and words' and actually completing their emerging written story! There are numerous ways that child authors can 'plot-plan' with ease as the suggestions below suggest!

Early Years Foundation Stage

- Make available tangible, open-ended resources (in a box or bag) to stimulate/ develop child authors' role play activity e.g. *a clock to signal a change from day-to night-time* or *a hat to indicate the arrival of a new character* (see http://tinyurl. com/33lgjrt for other ideas). Support child authors in talking about and then mark making/writing what happened in their role play 'after-the-event', presenting this as an emerging story e.g. *they go for a ride on a Glitter Bug* or *they nibble on some edible Silly String!*
- Invite child authors to draw/paint a picture which captures the 'goings-on' in an emerging story set in the outdoor play area e.g. *a pedal falls off James' tricycle* or *Sharondeep wins the kiss-chase race*. Support child authors in mark making/writing on strips of paper to 'tell the tale' in written form, displaying these on washing lines or floor displays alongside the completed pictures.

Key stage 1

- Explain to child authors what a visual storyboard is – 'a series of uncomplicated pictures that highlight the main ideas and turning points [of a story]' (Hiles *et al.*, 2008: 11) – and how this tool is used by movie makers (think Aardman Animation films). Support child authors in using one to visually represent the *start–middle–end* of an emerging 'slimy' story: '*What makes the story a "slimy" one – is it about worms, eels, snails/slugs or glorious green goo?*'
- Encourage child authors to sketch out the outline of a hill/Christmas tree/volcano/hat (witch/wizard)/pyramid/rollercoaster/triangle which all serve

as a representational adaption of the classic *Story Mountain* (see http://tinyurl.com/lhdfqn9). Support child authors in using their outline to plot the 'fundamental pattern to narrative' (Corbett, 2003: 10) to write a 'shock' story where all of the biscuits in the world have been eaten, Daddy starts talking backwards (*backwards talking starts he, yes!*) or the supply teacher for the day turns out to be a pelican!

Gold star!

Many busy professionals rely on the internet to find online resources/ideas to support/enrich their taught delivery and the learning experience of their child authors. Recommended quality sites linked to storytelling and storymaking (EYFS) and story planning (KS1) include:

EYFS	http://tinyurl.com/7wqlt5k	http://tinyurl.com/p9zjc9z
KS1	http://tinyurl.com/kfvsfje	http://tinyurl.com/p2gjug2

Think of a theme!

Martin (2011) highlights that there is a difference between *theme* and *thematic category*:

Item	Explanation	Example(s)
Thematic category	Universal experiences that every child could relate to	Friendship, Growing up, Sharing
Theme	Expression of what the author is trying to say *about* a thematic category	Friendship: 'A child can find friendship when she learns to give it'

In essence, '[t]he fully expressed theme tells us what the story is about on a philosophical level. It reflects a philosophy of the author' (ibid.). The ideas offered below are designed to support child authors in developing an emerging *understanding* of thematic categories and themes and how they can positively influence and enrich their emerging story mark making/writing.

Early Years Foundation Stage

- *Bedtime routines:* Read *Along Came a Bedtime* (Whybrow, 2008). Invite child authors to talk about their own bedtime routine. Encourage them to then 'mix it up' e.g. *brushing their teeth in bed, reading a book while putting on their pyjamas* or *putting Dolly in the bath!* Support them in mark making/writing an emerging story that reminds them that having an organised routine for bedtime is important!
- *Manners:* Read *Say Hello to the Dinosaurs!* (Whybrow, 2009). Identify dinosaurs in the book which you assert are really shy/ignorant/lazy/unfriendly and so they will not say 'Hello!' back if child authors ever greeted them. Get child authors to

mark make/write an emerging story about why we should always be courteous and polite to others: *it is nys 2 bee nys*. ('It is nice to be nice.' Greg, 4.10 yrs, independent writing.)

Key stage 1

- *Family and travel:* Read *King and King and family* (De Haan and Nijland, 2004). Encourage child authors to talk about places they have visited with their (step) family e.g. *day trips, weekends away* and *holidays*. Invite them to 'write up' one of these occasions as a short story, using aliases rather than the names of (step) family members. Talk with them as they work about the value of being open to new experiences with people that they love/care for.
- *Tears and crying:* Read *The Tear Thief* (Duffy, 2007). Suggest child authors mime incidences when they have 'shed a tear' – *can their peers/professionals correctly guess what caused them to cry?* Offer child authors blue teardrop-shaped paper on which they can write a story based on the title *The Day of Tears*, highlighting the fact that everyone cries e.g. *Dads at football matches when their team loses, Mums at romantic movies* and *siblings when they stub their toe*, and it is okay and natural to do so!

Gold star!

Display resources can be a powerful way to support child authors' emerging story mark making/writing. Visit http://tinyurl.com/m4tbbvq, *browsing* through the *Writing* resources for EYFS and KS1 for any useful ideas. Personal favourites include the *Writing Checklist* (EYFS) and the *KS1 Whole Body Writing Poster*. Also visit http://tinyurl.com/o7jgphc for a wealth of downloadable story writing prompts and aids for use in the setting/classroom in the form of posters, cards, mats, dice, signs and banners. Embrace these as valuable strategies to enrich your own display provision in the setting/classroom.

Tinkering with tales!

As a child, personal enjoyment was sought from writing stories that were based on those already known. The ability to 'tinker' with aspects of these tales, such as adapting characters' names, locations and dialogue, allowed 'my stories' to be created. Corbett (2008b: 2) refers to this as *innovation*, the second step of the storymaking process, and is a practice used by many storytellers such as Dargin (1996). Encourage child authors to mark make/write emerging stories by *innovating* known tales with a range of what are personally regarded as 'tinkering tools', as advocated by Corbett.

Early Years Foundation Stage – Tinkering Tool: Substitution

- Get child authors to identify the main characters in simple traditional stories e.g. *Little Red Riding Hood* and *The Gingerbread Man*. Suggest that they substitute these with different names e.g. *Sally* or *Biscuit Boy*, retelling the story in written form with marks/writing and drawings.

- Help child authors to recognise key locations or objects in known stories e.g. *Dear Zoo* (Campbell, 2010) or Eddy's teddy in *Where's My Teddy?* (Alborough, 2004). Support child authors in substituting these locations/objects with those that have meaning to them e.g. *a pet shop* (owned by the child author's parents), *a dolly*, *a farm* or *a trike*. Use these to tinker with repeated phrases in the new story e.g. *Wes Tommy* ('Where's Tommy?' Tommy, 4.10 yrs, independent writing).

Key stage I – Tinkering Tool: Additions

- Model how child authors can keep 'the same basic pattern and sentences' of the known story but can add in simple additions to 'embellish the original' (Corbett, 2008a: 4) by adding in *new characters* or *events* e.g. introducing a badger to *The Gruffalo* 'cast' (Donaldson, 1999) or getting Little Owl and Mummy to look for Daddy Owl (Haughton, 2013). Present these additions in the form of a 'new and improved' written story.
- Encourage child authors to add more *description* and *detail* to story sentences in their written story to enrich the content, composing the sentence orally before writing it down e.g. 'Yesterday I woke up with a jump and saw Bob the old cat crawling around MY BEDROOM, licking MY JAZZY PRINCESS JEWELLERY… so I shouted: GET OUT OF MY ROOM NOW! and that was the start of MY BIG SHOUTING DAY!' (adapted from Patterson, 2012).

Gold star!

Engage reluctant male child authors by offering them interesting resources to mark make/write their emerging stories with/on e.g. those used by *cavemen* (sticks in wet clay slabs), *medieval monks* (quills on parchment), *Egyptians* (bamboo reed pens on made papyrus) and *astronauts* (pencils on NASA headed paper). Consider stimulating the writing environment as well with relevant background music, costumes and 'levels' at which male child authors can write at e.g. *on the floor*, *on the wall*, *upside down* (lying on their back, writing upwards on a clipboard with pencils) or *on raised stands*. Also see http://tinyurl.com/k993yzz for research into stimulating children's imaginative writing using a virtual reality environment.

Plenty of prompts!

Unless children are natural child authors their mind is likely to 'draw a blank' when faced with a piece of paper/computer screen that they have to fill with an emerging story. The use of prompts to kick-start and support the emerging writing process has been the subject of interesting research (Graves *et al.*, 1994) with numerous authors using them, along with exercise, sleep and cold showers, to help break through their dreaded 'writer's block' (Smith, 1982). The suggestions below cover select prompts (underlined) to help child authors fill that page/screen!

Early Years Foundation Stage

- One of the simplest and most readily available prompts for child authors are story books. Use these with questions to prompt the extension of favourite stories ('*What did the Very Hungry Caterpillar nibble on after he became a beautiful butterfly?*'), different endings to a story (by only reading the first half of a story – '*How do you think the story will end?*') and the creation of new emerging stories ('*What could happen to Miffy today?*').
- Use toys that child authors play with in the setting as visual prompts for their emerging story mark making/writing e.g. a large box ('*Who lives in it?*'), a hat ('*What happens when it is worn?*') or a ball ('*What do you think it would say if it could talk?*').

Key stage I

- Visit http://tinyurl.com/yehg5gc for some exciting story prompts in the form of opening story sentences e.g. *Bob stopped to let the penguins cross the road. They were on their way to...* Print these out, making them freely available in the *Writers' Room* role play area in the classroom for child authors to select, adapt and use to 'open' their story.
- Play wordless music in the background as child authors write as an auditory prompt for their stories (Carter, 2012) – think about playing the theme tune to the *Indiana Jones* films as the children write an adventure story! See http://tinyurl.com/q4gdexf for further information. Alternatives include sound effects (*on CDs* or *those self-made/recorded*), auditory signals (*mobile ringtones* or *a hand-held bell*) and natural sounds (*birds singing* or *waves lapping on the shore*).

Gold star!

Visit http://tinyurl.com/8n998ee for a child-friendly, interactive website called *Story Starters* which 'inspire[s] students to write by serving up hundreds of writing prompts in creative combinations'. There are four *Story Starter* themes child authors and professionals can choose from: *Adventure, Fantasy, Sci-Fi* and *Scrambler*; the prompts are also differentiated by age. Click on the *Teachers' Guide* for some stimulating ideas on how to use the website in the setting/classroom as a whole group/focused group/paired/individual activity.

What if...?

Painter (in Bernays and Painter, 1990: xvi) claims that '[w]riting exercises have long been a part of the learning process for new and established writers'. One such exercise is generating *What Ifs* – questions that have the potential to fuel an entire story (see

What If? Shipton, 1999). The creative possibilities of *What Ifs* for emerging story writing are seemingly endless – professionals only have to visit http://tinyurl.com/n5tsbhl for a truly wonderful example to see what *What Ifs* could do for the emerging story writing of your child authors!

Early Years Foundation Stage

- Present the following *What Ifs* in picture form on different pieces of card: *What if you could draw with your nose/breathe underwater/walk upside down/cook with four arms/talk with your teddy?* Invite child authors to select a card, 'playing out' what they would do if they could do what is on the card. Get them to mark make/write down one of their ideas as an entry for 'The Most Creative *What If* Emerging Story Competition'!
- Wilson (2012) advocates asking child authors *What if you woke up this morning and a cuddly lion cub was sleeping at the foot of your bed?* or *What if everything you touched turned to chocolate?* '[C]ontinue to ask Who, What, When, Where, Why and How questions until they begin to see a story forming.' Work with individual child authors to capture this emerging story in both written and picture form using appropriately shaped/coloured pieces of paper associated with the tale e.g. *bed-shaped* or *chocolate bar-shaped*.

Key stage 1

- Present different *What Ifs* in a large chalked hopscotch grid on the playground e.g. *What if your imaginary friend became real/your school pumps kept running away from you/you could not be seen or heard by anybody because you were a ghost/you lived in the ocean or a video game?* Get child authors to throw a stone – whichever *What If* it lands on should serve as the inspiration for their written story which could be presented inside an A4 paper hopscotch grid.
- Bevan (2007) shows the potential of *What Ifs* in stimulating story writing with reference to a wonderful collection of topics – *The day our teacher was ill, Curious catalogues, Peculiar pets, Every picture tells a story, Fairground fun, A postcard home*. Visit http://tinyurl.com/nkcb8sx, encouraging child authors to select a topic and a *What If* as the basis of their own written story.

Gold star!

Defined as 'a pivotal moment in your life guided by a seemingly insignificant decision or random act of fate that changes you' (see http://tinyurl.com/k6rzk5e), invite child authors to mark make/write an *If/Then* story: *'if this happened then this would happen...'* Suggest that child authors *build on* experiences in their life using *What Ifs* e.g. *What if you walked to the shops rather than going by car?* Then (EYFS) or *What if you took a different path through the woods to Aunty Margie's house?* Then (KS1).

Glorious game play!

Wenner (2009) asserts that there is a 'serious need' for children to play, a sentiment well supported by those who work in the EYFS! For those in KS1 it is more difficult to offer what is considered to be the most essential type of play for children – imaginative and rambunctious [noisy, exuberant, wild] 'free play' – due to pressures on the timetable, the demands of the curriculum and the target-driven agenda which continues to shape the practices of professionals in the primary sector. So how is it possible to combine play and emerging story writing, particularly in KS1? The answer is *game play*!

Early Years Foundation Stage

- Introduce child authors to a new puppet e.g. a bunny. Invite them to ask 'Ben the Bunny' questions to find out something about him e.g. *What is his favourite food? Where does he live? What does he like to play with?* Suggest that child authors draw/write an emerging story involving Ben by basing it around something they now know e.g. *the day Ben's pet hamster stole his carrot* or *the 'play date' with Betsie, Bunny's best friend at his burrow.*
- Encourage child authors to experiment with different face paints (under close supervision!) As they create get them to talk about possible things their new character could get up to. Work with them to draw/mark make/write about one of these ideas as an emerging story e.g. *the princess spills red juice on her evening gown* or *the messy builder builds a Lego house for one of the Three Little Pigs.*

Key stage I

- Get two child authors (number them 1 and 2) to sit opposite one another with a barrier (a board, a big book or a curtain) between them. Invite child author 1 to read aloud a short story they have written involving helicopters, ponies or a talking sofa; child author 2 must listen and draw a picture in response to what happens in the story. Get child author 2 to show child author 1 their drawing – *how does it compare to what child author 1 visually had in their mind?* Talk together about how child author 1 might improve their story – *more description? More explicit detail about characters and settings? How might this help to improve the drawings of child author 2?*
- Offer child authors a board on which is drawn a grid (5×5 squares) – in each square there is written/printed a different word e.g. *house, bath, sock, car, phone, dog, music, park* and *TV.* Ask child authors to throw a di(c)e and toss that number of counters over the board – wherever the counters land child authors must strive to integrate these words in their creative story about the funny-tasting morning!

Gold star!

At the start of the educational year suggest that Literacy Co-ordinators invest a little of their budget in one of the following practical books which offers a wealth of exciting activities to stimulate storytelling, storymaking and story games for child authors of different ages:

Age group	Title (publisher, year of publication)	Author
EYFS	*Planning for the Early Years: Storytelling and Storymaking* (Practical PreSchool Books, 2012)	Judith Stevens
	Stories: Ages 3–5 (Belair Publications, 2012)	Pat Gain
KS1	*The Bumper Book of Story Telling into Writing at Key stage 1* (Clown Publishing, 2006)	Pie Corbett
	Storyteller: Traditional Stories to Read, Tell and Write (Scholastic, 2008)	Pie Corbett

Writing in role!

In an effort to create context for children's emerging writing, Schneider and Jackson (2000) advocate the use of process drama. While there are many forms of this e.g. *Reader's Theatre* and *Mantle of the Expert*, this Idea will focus on *Writing in Role*. The benefits of encouraging child authors to mark make/write as a character/different person are evident in the research findings of Cremin *et al.* (2006: 273): '[I]n addition to a palpable increase in motivation and commitment, an enhanced sense of focus, flow and ease in [children's] writing was noticeable.' So...*how can this be used to stimulate child authors' emerging story writing?* Please see below!

Early Years Foundation Stage

- Get child authors to select one of their favourite story characters e.g. *Little Tiger*, *Pirate Pete* or *Maisy*. Sprinkle some invisible 'magic dust' over them, turning them into the creative *author* or *illustrator* of these characters. Invite them to mark make/write a new emerging story involving their beloved character. *'What will happen in the new story? Will it be a sad/happy/funny/crazy story? Might it be about a shopping trip, a ride in a "special" vehicle or a poorly day?'*
- In the hospital role play area get child authors to write-in-role as a *visitor* who mark makes/writes an emerging story to help cheer up a bed-ridden patient they have come to see. Encourage them to make the story fun and exciting e.g. 'Mummy's toilet took off to the seaside!' (Story dictation, Kyle, 3.6 yrs.)

Key stage I

- Get female child authors to pretend to be *Rapunzel*. In an effort to while away the hours in the ivory tower, suggest that she writes a short story about an adventure she imagines having with the prince once she escapes from the enchantress. For male child authors, get them write-in-role as the *Prince*, writing an imaginary adventure story involving Rapunzel as he waits for the silk ladder to be finished – think *scuba diving, searching for the ScuttleBug* or *time travelling to the Stone Age*.

- 'Set the scene' by getting child authors to imagine they are an *exhausted mum or dad* whose baby/toddler is struggling to get to sleep! Tell them that the story books Mum/Dad have borrowed in haste from the library are not appropriate (show them story books with wild illustrations and lots of words) so Mum/Dad resort to quickly jotting down their own short story to soothe their baby/toddler. *What do they write about?* Offer child authors examples of published bedtime stories for young children as stimuli to help them with the language, characters, plot, illustrations and ending e.g. *they were all very, very tired and so went to sleep – Goodnight!*

Gold star!

Sentence strips are a valuable resource for story building (see http://tinyurl.com/l5v5byo and Morris, 1993). 'Energise' the use of these in the setting/classroom by coiling blank sentence strips up into *Super Story Snails* which can be used to stimulate child authors' emerging story mark making (EYFS) and extend their simple story sentences (KS1). Alternatives include bending the strip into an arch to create a *Super Story Rainbow* or folding the strip back and forth on itself to create a *Super Story Zig-Zag Caterpillar*. Undertake a web search for further sentence strips activities to use with your child authors in an effort to further energise their use in the setting/classroom.

Who am I writing this for?

The research	Research by Tamburrini *et al.* (1984) sought to develop an understanding of children's sense of audience in their writing.
What the research found	They found that 'the vast output of writing in schools[/settings] was written almost entirely for teachers[/professionals]' (p. 195).
Implications for practice	Child authors should be encouraged to write emerging stories for a *wide range* of readers, not just for those who are going to mark it!

So, who might these 'wide range of readers' be? Suggestions include:

Early Years Foundation Stage	*Key stage 1*
• Themselves • Those who are close to the child author e.g. *siblings, pets, friends* and *teddy/toys* • Parents/carers	• Peers • Family members e.g. *cousins, uncles* and *aunties* • Other professionals e.g. *Headteachers, cleaners, midday supervisors* and *governors*

Those who child authors come into contact with on a daily/weekly basis could also serve as interesting audiences for their emerging story mark making/writing e.g. *child minders, private day care providers, breakfast/after-school providers, sports leaders, Brownie/Beavers/Cub leaders, music/dance teachers* and *shop owners*. More unusual audiences include *visitors to the setting, hospital patients, royalty* (think Baby

Charlotte), *invisible friends*, *toys* (think *Toy Story*), *pets* (see Paradise, 2007), *future generations* (putting emerging written stories in a story time-capsule that is buried in the grounds of the setting/school), *employers of parents/carers*, *characters associated with yearly events* e.g. Christmas (*Father Christmas*) and Easter (*the Easter Bunny*), *authors of children's books* e.g. Julia Donaldson, *future girlfriends/boyfriends*, *the elderly* and *those who have passed on* e.g. grandparents. Help child authors to select from this wealth of writing audiences for their emerging stories by using the following strategies:

EYFS		KS1	
	Ask child authors to verbally identify who they would like to write their emerging story for.		Have images of different writing audiences on pieces of card. Get child authors to select a card purely at random.
	Ask peers to select an audience for them all to write for or just their friend to write for.		Get child authors to select one of the writing audience cards for one of their peers to write for.

It is important for child authors to not only be aware of *who* they are writing their emerging stories for but also *why* they are writing for them. It is suggested that there are between three and four main purposes of writing stories: to *inform*, to *entertain* and to *educate*. When child authors initiate work on their emerging stories support them in considering the reason(s) for mark making/writing for their targeted audience, ensuring that this serves as an underlying 'driving force' for the emerging story being told; this can also act as a useful way of evaluating the quality of their emerging story mark making/writing as older child authors can ask those who read their work (if possible and appropriate) what they 'took' from their story once they have finished it: *What do they know now that they did not know before? Were they 'engaged' when reading the story – why/not? What might/will they do as a result of reading their story?* This information could also be sought in written form, as appropriate.

Gold star!

Encourage older child authors to consider different ways to present their emerging stories for their readers e.g.:

- on paper or card;
- using ICT applications e.g. simple word processing packages, PowerPoint slides, video recordings and digital images (photographs); and
- as a piece of audio using a microphone or a dictation machine.

This will influence the way in which older child authors' emerging stories are received by their targeted audience e.g.:

- being physically handed to them;
- sent either using the postal system (stories written on paper or electronically burnt onto a rewritable CD); and
- through electronic means (email attachments, sound files, weblinks).

Alternatively, child authors could read it out to their target audience by inviting them into the setting/classroom or going and reading it to their audience elsewhere in the setting/school/local area.

Expert advice!

As a child author I can vividly recollect being visited at my primary school by a local poet (Jan Perry) who shared her 'words of wisdom' about writing with my classmates and then read a poem she had written about 'magical' me (I still have the poem!)! There are many wonderful writers and professionals who have real expertise in the field of story writing and education. This Idea celebrates the incredible 'theory and practice' of select educationalists, sharing quality ideas to develop and enrich story mark making/writing practices with your child authors.

Early Years Foundation Stage

- Stevens (2012: 10) advocates the notion of pick-and-mix stories: a 'story [that] gives children the opportunity to choose characters, locations and artefacts and use them to create their own story'. Offer child authors collections of toy characters (small world), images of locations (pictures, photos) and 'interesting familiar and unfamiliar objects', selecting one of each as the basis for a short verbalised story that is then written down (with support) for posterity purposes.
- Clarke and Featherstone (2008: 39) promote the idea of children 'writing everywhere'. Encourage child authors to mark make/write emerging stories in different learning areas in the setting, accessing portable writing equipment found in 'small baskets...backpacks... writing belts [and] small trolleys' so that child authors can 'write [while] on the move'.

Key stage I

- Rosen (in Corbett, 2003: 27) offers a wealth of strategies for innovating (altering) well-known tales: '1, Take bits out... 2, Add bits in... 3, Change things... 4, Extract the underlying plot.' Encourage child authors to utilise one or more of these strategies in their own emerging story writing, playing around with events, characters, descriptions, dialogue, settings, and openings and endings in an effort to create their own *magnum opus*!

- Wright (1997: 82) proposes the idea of bare-bones stories where 'you tell a very simple story and the children [seek answers to] questions to make it richer and more interesting'. Offer child authors a 'story skeleton' – *'The man walks along the road'* (p. 82) or *'A girl looks for her cat. She asks, "Where is my cat?" She finds it.'* (p. 83) – encouraging them to ask a series of who/what/where/how/why/when questions to expand the tale in both verbal and then written form.

Gold star!

Haloin *et al.* (2005) have compiled a valuable grid which details characteristics associated with different genres of text. Visit http://tinyurl.com/956mbo8, considering using this as a professional resource to develop one's own/child authors' subject knowledge (as appropriate) about story types, strengthen direct teaching points, shape success criteria, or positively influence emerging story writing provision and practice. Older child authors could be encouraged to practise writing quick and simple genre checklists prior to their story writing as this can help them to remember the key features/elements and develop structure and coherence in their tales.

Story writing 'pick and mix' 7

Here is a seventh collection of stimulating story writing ideas to engage child authors and enrich professional practices. As explained in 'Story writing "pick and mix" 1' (see p. 23) this assortment of ideas is not attributed to a particular age phase but is offered more as a selection of suggestions for professionals to choose from and adapt in response to the mark making/writing needs of their learners – *put an 'X' by any that you think you might try out!*

X
↓

Sewing story: Offer child authors a folded piece of coloured paper which has holes punched down both sides *of the crease* that runs down the middle of the page. Invite them to mark make / trace / write individual words or single sentences that collectively tell an emerging story, presenting them in a random order over the page *in line* with each of the different holes. Pass the story to a peer with a long piece of wool for them to literally 'sew' the story sentence / tale together in the right order.

Story slide: Talk to child authors about a rather unusual slide at the park – any child who goes down it disappears off the end of it for a day! *'Where do they end up? What do they do there? Who do they meet? How do they get back home?'* Decisions, decisions…!

'Shut it' story: Get child authors to open the start of an emerging written story using British comedian Larry Grayson's famous catchphrase: *'Shut that door!'* But what are they shutting the door on? Snow? Monsters? An advancing army? The wind? An apologising friend? The rain? An animal (e.g. a bear)? Consider presenting the written story on a piece of paper with a door-shape flap cut out of it.

Shining story: Challenge child authors to write an emerging story about a character who is given the chance to 'shine' e.g. *save someone's life, sing for charity, rescue a cat* or *bravely stand up to a peer's bully.* Provide them with a torch, shining this behind and into the paper that the story is presented on to illuminate the words of the distinguished!

ABC story: Invite older child authors to write a short story in which there is at least one word which starts with a different letter of the alphabet. Variations on this idea include the following.

- At least one word in the story must *end* with a different letter of the alphabet (both conventional and reverse ordering).
- Write part of the story (or at least one sentence) with the alphabet sequence guiding the word order e.g. *Andy bought Carrie's dad every florescent golf hat in Jenny's kiosk. Larry…*

Story website: Visit http://tinyurl.com/lvydvh8 for some varied learning and teaching strategies for professionals to add to their emerging story writing teaching toolkit, adapting and modelling these to suit the needs and abilities of child authors that you work with.

Chapter 8

Resourcing the story stimulation!

Pictures and photographs!

Open any non-fiction book for young children and readers are likely to be overwhelmed with visual stimuli in the form of pictures and photographs that support the printed text. Armes (2009) asserts that these '[g]raphics are great for stimulating new [creative writing] ideas'. These graphics can come in the form of *real art work*, *digital images*, *hand-drawn illustrations*, *reproductions*, *printed snapshots* and *postcards*. With support from professionals, child authors can use these as inspiration for their emerging stories!

Early Years Foundation Stage

- Invite child authors to take photographs around the setting using child-friendly digital cameras. View these as a small group on the IWB, selecting one as the stimulus for an emerging 'rummaging' story in which child authors search for objects that begin with a particular phoneme or, even better, hidden treasure e.g. 'We found rough marbles in the sandpit!' (Story dictation, Hassan, 3.6 yrs.)
- It is well established that young children learn to read by initially telling stories based on wordless picture books. Offer child authors 'the opportunity to write the text to a wordless book' (Marron, 2010: 3) by using marks, letters, words and dictated simple sentences. Record this text either on paper strips that can be temporarily attached to pages in the book that relate to the relevant illustrations or on clear acetate sheets that can be paper-clipped to the page.

Key stage 1

- Offer child authors a small selection of Jindrich's (2014) *Story Starters* illustrations. Invite them to select one and, with a partner, talk about the illustration in terms of the character(s) and setting. Support them in creating a simple narrative which *builds on* the illustration by modelling how to develop a simple *plot*, a little *conflict* and a story *resolution* through critical questioning and creative thinking strategies – see http://tinyurl.com/qcb2kql and http://tinyurl.com/nh2o3nq for ideas and suggestions.
- Challenge child authors to find a printed photograph in a celebrity magazine, be it an advert or a paparazzi-taken picture. Get them to cut this out and glue it onto

a large piece of paper, writing a short story literally *around* it based on the captured action e.g. shopping (*for what and why?*), talking on the phone (*to whom and what about?*) or looking at a watch (*time for what?*).

Gold star!

There are many wonderful online resources and published texts available to support professionals and child authors in using pictures and photographs as prompts for emerging story writing. Recommended materials include the picture prompt cards (three sets) from *SparkleBox* (see http://tinyurl.com/nv4y249) (EYFS) and the work of Carter (2012) (KS1). Explore these with colleagues, considering the value of adding or adapting these materials to enhance current provision and practice. Other resources and ideas can be found at http://tinyurl.com/q53casq.

Paintings and drawings!

The J. Paul Getty Trust (n.d.) puts it beautifully when it states that

> [w]orks of art often tell stories. Artists can present narrative in many ways – by using a series of images representing moments in a story, or by selecting a central moment to stand for the whole story. Narrative works often illustrate well-known historical, religious, legendary or mythic stories. Sometimes, however, artists invent their own stories, leaving the viewer to imagine the narrative.

With the support of professionals, young child authors can capitalise on the creative story potential that is seemingly so richly provided by paintings and drawings!

Early Years Foundation Stage

- Display on a washing line images of famous paintings by the likes of Kandinsky, Miró, Monet, Klee, Picasso and Pollock. Get child authors to pretend they visit one of these artists and collaborate together with them on a new painting! Invite them to create their new masterpiece with various painting resources, mark making/writing an emerging story about their exciting day together: 'We dribbled paint on the floor!' (Story dictation, Edgar, 3.8 yrs.)
- Visit http://tinyurl.com/kqhqvjr, using the activity described by Stewart (2013) as the basis for some individual/small group 'coloured crayon' storytelling, encouraging child authors to mark make/write under their drawings to capture their emerging story in written form. Consider reading *The Day The Crayons Quit* (Daywalt, 2013) as further inspiration.

Key stage 1

- Visit http://tinyurl.com/ozkjnty, selecting the most well-known of the six artists available – *Vincent Van Gogh*. Focus on the screen depicting the painting *Starry Night*, asking child authors if they have 'ever made a picture of a dream'. Challenge them to capture one of their dreams (real/imagined) on paper, imitating Van Gogh's unique thick brushstrokes and use of vivid colours. Get them to write a simple narrative to tell the story of the dream that can be orally read to an art lover (Mum perhaps?) or someone who is sight impaired from the local community.
- Goularte (2014 – see http://tinyurl.com/ml4vby8) offers a wonderful sequence of freely available lessons and resources to get child authors drawing and writing. Consider adapting these materials to cater for the specific needs of the child authors you work with, thinking about your expectations of them in terms of their writing, levels of support to be given (physical/prompt sheets), the wordless picture book to be selected and the intended outcomes of the stories that they write.

Gold star!

Huff (2000: 6) advocates the use of puppets, props and story corners to stimulate 'playful tales'. Support child authors of all ages in making and using box/finger/folded paper/glove/hand/stick/tube puppets and story walls/aprons/waistcoats/boxes/cubes/cans/bags in an effort to 'stimulate imaginations… develop oral communication skills…[and] create a love of books, reading and, eventually, writing' (ibid.). See http://tinyurl.com/ovu3ba9 and http://tinyurl.com/npmcch7 for practical support in making story puppets, seeking online support for making, creating and using props and story corners.

Colours and shapes!

Church (2014) acknowledges 'two very noticeable attributes of the world around us': colour and shape, recognition of both which form part of all children's core learning. As there are numerous children's story books linked to colour (see http://tinyurl.com/l43ns4n) and published compilations of shape poetry available (see Foster, 2005), child authors should be positively encouraged to utilise the creative potential that colours and shapes can offer their own emerging story mark making/writing (with support from professionals, of course)!

Early Years Foundation Stage

- Encourage child authors to look carefully at the printed writing in their favourite story books. *'What colour is the text?'* (typically **black**). Invite them to mark make/write an emerging story in which they 'seek out' different coloured objects in the setting, mark making/writing the text using a coloured crayon/pencil that matches the item that they found e.g. *i fb a reb dl* ('I found a red ball', Henry, 4.5 yrs, guided writing).

- Offer child authors malleable materials for them to manipulate into thin (flat) recognisable shapes e.g. *a heart, a doughnut* (ring) or *the sun* (circle). Add these as sensory illustrations to their emerging story mark making/writing associated with their chosen shape e.g. *the snack time they got a doughnut stuck on their finger* or *going on a sunny holiday in a huge bumper/water/roller/zorb ball!*

Key stage I

- Read *My Many Coloured Days* (Seuss, 2001). Suggest that child authors write a 'Day-In-The-Life' story about a character on coloured paper which represents their mood e.g. *red = angry* (see http://tinyurl.com/6z2o5ys for support). Support child authors in carefully 'matching' their character's mood to their speech and actions e.g. *happy (yellow): 'What a lovely day!'/skipping and singing.*
- Invite child authors to go on a shape hunt in around the classroom/school (see http://tinyurl.com/qa9blzb for a useful PDF). Encourage child authors to number the shapes in the order in which they find them. Use this as a 'story sequencer' for a written story in which they discover these different shapes in fantasy-based settings e.g. 'I saw a sparklie star in dark spayce' (Jessica, 5.10 yrs).

Gold star!

Colourful Stories is described as 'a visual support strategy which helps children to learn about the structure of stories and become more confident about telling and writing stories'. Created by Elks and McLachlan (2013 – see http://tinyurl. com/ppe6spf), this resource can be used by professionals and parents/carers with children in the EYFS and KS1. Visit the website for more information, considering the value of utilising this as a new strategy to support emerging story mark making/writing in the setting/classroom. Alternatively, read about 'Colourful stories' (Rylands, 2008) that were created by children in EYFS and KS1 via the use of *2Create A Story*, a simple piece of computer software which could become a useful addition to your software collection.

Newspapers and magazines!

Research into children's reading habits suggests that 'more [girls and] young people from White backgrounds read magazines...and more [boys and] young people from Black backgrounds read...newspapers' (Clark, 2011: 5). With many child authors coming into regular contact with newspapers and magazines in a variety of different contexts – think *their home, the setting/classroom* and *in the doctor's/dentist's waiting room* – professionals should be encouraged to help child authors to see these as a 'sizzling source of potential' that can invigorate their emerging story writing.

Early Years Foundation Stage

- Give child authors a story book that has been wrapped up in a piece of newspaper or a magazine page. Invite them to predict what they think the story is about. Get them to mark make/write their emerging 'predictive story' with support before opening their wrapped story (to initially stimulate thinking encourage child authors to progressively tear off small pieces of the paper to 'reveal' part of the cover. *'Any ideas now?'*). Support them in talking about how similar/different the two stories are once the book has been revealed.

- Get child authors to cut out a couple of pictures of different people (photographs/drawings) from a newspaper or a magazine, sticking these onto a large piece of sugar paper. Support them in thinking up a simple emerging story which involves the two individuals, mark making/writing their story underneath e.g. *the two of them go to the beach, they go sailing on a star, they skate together over a frozen strawberry milkshake lake* or *they sing with their favourite pop/TV stars.*

Key stage 1

- Show child authors an advertisement from a magazine for a story-writing competition. Invite child authors to submit a written story for a *class* story-writing competition based around a particular topic e.g. *Friendship, Pets, Disappointment, Wishes* or *The Natural World.* Consider adapting the prompts found on pp. 89–101 of *501 Writing Prompts* (LearningExpress, 2003) for additional topics. Ensure that child authors are aware of what the adjudicating panel (you, colleagues, local authors) are looking for in terms of the winning submission, linking this to key writing success criteria (see http://tinyurl.com/khgu54z for adaptable suggestions).

- Share with child authors simple (and age-appropriate) headlines from newspapers and magazines. Support them in thought showering their 'story potential' by getting them to collaborate in pairs to write a story inspired by a particular title e.g. *Magician Saves Birthday Boy's Life!* could be about a dozy child magician who resuscitates the angry birthday boy from choking to death on a piece of 'lit' Buzz Lightyear birthday cake!

Gold star!

A valuable way to improve child authors' emerging story mark making/writing and to develop professional practice is in response to findings and recommendations. These are likely to be influenced and shaped by government policy, research reports and literacy organisation guidance. Choose from one of the following web links, considering the findings and recommendations offered, and how practical suggestions could be adapted and integrated into your existing provision:

http://tinyurl.com/nak7fju   http://tinyurl.com/ormzjox   http://tinyurl.com/nqq26tm

Music and sounds!

DeNora (2000) asserts that music helps to create an environment which is good for concentrating and focusing – personal reflections note that this entire book was written while music was playing in the background! Disney's *Fantastia* and Prokofiev's *Peter and the Wolf* serve as two well-known examples of how classical music has been used to stimulate storytelling; one only has to hear the sound of a descending glissando (a rapid sliding down of the musical scale) from a slide whistle to imagine someone or something falling down or over! With support from professionals child authors can learn the true potential of music and sounds in helping to stimulate their emerging stories!

Early Years Foundation Stage

- Get child authors in a small quiet space (*corridor* or *hall*), telling them a short story in a hushed voice about a family (*human/animal*) who are all asleep in the dead of night. Describe how everything is still, quiet and uneventful until **SUDDENLY** [offer them the musical instrument box] **AN ENORMOUS NOISE WAKES EVERYONE UP!** Get them to mark make/write an emerging story about *who* is making the noise – *Monsters? The twin babies? Mice?* – and how different family members react to the noise e.g. with *screams*, *shouts*, *banged heads*, *falling down the stairs*, *laughter* and *dancing*.
- Read favourite stories to child authors at Story Time, encouraging them to add 'mouthed' sound effects or body percussion where appropriate e.g. *the wind 'blowing'*, *the 'creaking' of a door* or *the 'chug-chug-chug' of the train*. Encourage them to replicate these noises during the mark making/writing of an emerging story designed to make Poorly Panda smile – *might there be some rude-sounding noises to make him chuckle perhaps?!*

Key stage 1

- Play child authors pieces of music from different genres which can evoke images in their minds with the support of professionals e.g. soundtracks (*Despicable Me 2*), theme tunes (*various Hanna-Barbera cartoons*) or pop songs (*Gangnam Style*). Encourage them to keep their eyes closed as they listen to the music. *What images are being painted in their mind as they listen?* Get them to sketch what they 'saw' on paper, using this as a stimulus for a short story. See Gilbert (2007) for an interesting essay on the influence of music on paintings and animation.
- Play musical sounds from behind a curtain/screen/board, getting child authors to distinguish what they are and what they represent. Suggest that they use one of these sounds as the opener for a written fantasy story, presenting the sound in big capital letters to immediately draw the reader into the tale e.g. *BANG! WHIZZ! CLIP CLOP! DING-A-LING-A-LING! Perhaps the main character always makes this sound – but why?*

Gold star!

EmpoweringWriters.com advocates the 'showing rather than telling' approach when writing about the reactions of story characters in response to their feelings. As child authors build in their emerging storytelling and mark making/writing confidence, encourage them to replace simple *tellings* – 'He was happy' – with simple *showings* of characters' feelings through facial and body movements e.g. 'smile on face...heart leaps...jump up and down...hands clasped together...eyes open wide.' See http://tinyurl.com/po52bnk for more examples. For young child authors use physical body positions and actions to exemplify 'showings', referring to relevant illustrations in picture books as well.

Songs and rhymes!

It is recognised by the likes of Parlakian and Lerner (2010: 17) that song lyrics and rhymes 'tell a story'. It would be a shame if child authors were not taught about the rich potential that songs they sing along to and rhymes that they can recite have for their emerging story writing; it is thus important that professionals not only actively *teach* children songs and rhymes as part of the curriculum but also show them how they can assist child authors in being creative and innovative emerging story mark makers/writers!

Early Years Foundation Stage

- Get child authors to have a little 'sing-song' together, joining in with their favourite nursery rhymes. Ask child authors to identify the main character(s) that are part of the 'story' in one of the rhymes e.g. *Jack and Jill*. Get them to think about where they might go the following day. *Up a mountain? Up a ladder? Up a beanstalk?* (see Evans, 2013). Mark make/write an emerging story about their new adventure using *Stone Stories* as possible inspiration (see http://tinyurl.com/meoynhh)!
- Sing simple songs that have much repetition in them e.g. *Old MacDonald*. Get child authors to stop at *'And on that farm he had –'*, encouraging them to 'switch on their thinking caps' and think of outrageous things that could be found on the farm e.g. *talking candles*, *aliens*, *alarm clocks* or *sparkly stars*. Invite them to mark make/write an emerging story about the day the candles/aliens/alarm clocks/stars disappeared. *'Where did they go, and why?'*

Key stage 1

- Refresh child authors' memories by singing different nursery rhymes (see http://tinyurl.com/k9w83a4 for support). Get them to write down the lyrics of one of these rhyme, replacing nouns/verbs/adjectives with different ones (get them to imagine they are a 'song doctor'). Use this as a reference point to write the rhyme up as an interesting story e.g. *Twinkle Twinkle Little Star* could become a tale

about a sparkling ring that falls off the Queen's finger and is gobbled up by one of her corgis (idea by Greg, 6.0 yrs). *'How does she get it back?'*
- The love of Disney songs is pretty much universal – just think of 'Let It Go' from *Frozen*! Get child authors to choose their favourite song from a Disney film, thinking carefully about the lyrics and what is actually being sung. Invite them to take a line and use this as the title or inspiration for a story e.g. 'You've won your own free pass' from 'Be Our Guest' (*Beauty and the Beast*): a pass to what? *A football match? A gala ball? A film premiere? Entry to a dungeon? 'What happens when the story character gets there – who does not want them there?'*

Gold star!

There is evidence to suggest that the story-writing skills of child authors can be developed through the use of ICT. Select one of the short stimulating readings offered below, considering the implications (notional/actual) that could be made to child authors' emerging story-writing performance through using more ICT applications and software in your setting/classroom:

Key stage	Title	Authors	Weblinks
EYFS	ICT in the Early Years: Balancing the risks and the benefits	Shah and Godiyal (n.d.)	http://tinyurl.com/qxubsmh
KS1	What the research says about using ICT in English	Becta (2003)	http://tinyurl.com/ly5w7v5

Animation and film!

The immense power of animation and film in stimulating and supporting emerging story writing cannot be underestimated; VIA University College (2013: 2) assert that '[u]sing animation as a tool to encourage and develop children's learning is not only fun but effective' in enriching 'skills and competencies [such as] storytelling [and] concentration'. With the potential to excite, engage and assist child authors, professionals should see animation and film as an essential pedagogical device for their emerging story mark making/writing 'toolkit'!

Early Years Foundation Stage

- Invite child authors to select a DVD from the setting's collection of animated 'shorts' e.g. *Paddington*, *Mr. Men* and *Little Miss*, *Looney Tunes* or *Tom and Jerry*. Suggest that they mark make/write a 'story slice' which focuses on just one part (the exciting bit) of an animated 'short' viewed. Once complete, get them to sit with peers and talk about the whole story with reference to their 'story slice'. Alternatively, see BFI (2007) as a visual source of inspiration.

- Show child authors the short scene from *The Lion, the Witch and the Wardrobe* where Lucy looks into the wardrobe (see http://tinyurl.com/np4f2wy). Stop the film just before Lucy steps into Narnia, getting child authors to guess what Lucy sees. Get child authors to use shoe/cardboard boxes as models of the wardrobe, creatively using small world resources and collage materials to 'show off' the magical land they believe Lucy steps into, developing oral and emerging written stories from this visual stimuli.

Key stage 1

- Show child authors *'Dustbin Robot' by Simon* (yes, I made this!) – see http://tinyurl.com/nuh9z5x. Get them to generate names for the Robot and the dustbin, verbalising speech and sounds that the characters might make while discussing ideas about where the dustbin went and what it did there after 'The End'. Encourage them to write either a story retelling of the animation viewed or a story sequel post the animated interaction between the two characters.
- Visit http://tinyurl.com/k5pw677 for a remarkable 'teaching guide to using film and television with three- to eleven-year olds' called *Look Again!* (BFI, 2003). Focus on Chapter 2 (pp. 7–13), considering how different teaching techniques can be used to develop aspects of child authors' story writing in response to observed film segments e.g. writing 'sensory descriptions' as part of a story short following an 'auditory viewing' (see *Sound and Image*, p. 9) of the films *Stuart Little* or *Home*. Alternatively, see *Starting Stories* (BFI, 2004).

Gold star!

While this book aims to offer professionals a wealth of stimulating strategies, ideas and tips for the setting/classroom it does not claim to be 'the definitive' resource for supporting emerging story writing. Consider investing in one of the following texts to supplement your own personal bank of story mark making/ writing suggestions:

EYFS	*How to Teach Story Writing Ages 4–7* (Corbett, 2015)	*The Little Book of Props for Writing* (Roberts, 2012)
KS1	*Funny Stories for Ages 5–7* (Braund and Gibbon, 2010) (one of a series of Writing Guides with CD-ROM)	*You Can Write A Story! A Story-Writing Recipe for Kids* (Bullard, 2007)

Toys and trinkets!

Children's love of toys is universal, and it is widely recognised that toys have an important part to play in their development, largely because 'their play is often influenced by the toys they use' (TRUCE, 2009–2010: 3). Children's stories such as *Corduroy*, *Pinocchio* and *The Velveteen Rabbit*, along with family movies such as *Toy Story* and *The Christmas Toy* highlight the real potential that toys have for stimulating child authors' emerging story mark making/writing, particularly if these toys are 'living'. This potential also applies to trinkets despite the very name suggesting 'a thing of little value'!

Early Years Foundation Stage

*   Invite child authors to bring their *smallest* stuffed toy from home to the setting. Encourage them to sit together at the mark making/writing table, talking about/drawing/mark making/writing an emerging story about the things they like *and would like* to do together e.g. 'I like cuddling Bingo at bedtime' (story dictation, Molly, 3.5 yrs).
*   Offer child authors a small collection of trinkets, allowing them to be shared out and handled. Get child authors to imagine that each trinket is magical. '*What could happen if you wear/use the trinket?*' Support child authors in talking about/drawing/mark making/writing about the magical effects of their chosen trinket e.g. *I. got. big.* ('I grew bigger', Sammy, 4.7 yrs, independent writing).

Key stage 1

*   Read *Mrs Armitage on Wheels* (Blake, 1999). Get child authors to write their own version of the story with themselves as the protagonist – *Master* or *Miss _____ on Wheels* – adding things to a different 'wheeled' item e.g. *skateboards*, *roller skates*, *tricycles* or *scooters*. Encourage them to use Blake's repetitive phrasing to help structure their own individual sentences: '*What this _____ really needs...*'
*   Show child authors examples of trinket boxes (real or web-based images). Challenge child authors to write a story about a character who one day secretly steals a trinket box that belongs to their Grandma. '*What's inside it? Anything soft/silly/unusual/sweet/old/strange/precious/smelly/beautiful? Why does Grandma keep these items in the trinket box? What happens when Grandma finds out the trinket box has been taken – is she happy/cross/angry/sad?*'

Gold star!

Visit http://tinyurl.com/crd4rc4 to find out all about *Story Strings*, Bowkett's (2010) wonderful story writing resource. Simple to make and use, Bowkett advocates the use of *Story Strings* in both KS1 and KS2. This idea can be easily adapted for children in the EYFS by attaching items (real/images of) to a long 'string' washing line to help promote simple story sequencing e.g. *straw, sticks, paper bricks* and *a pot* for the story of *The Three Little Pigs*. Also see http://tinyurl.com/ladctj6.

Random inspiration!

Allen (2010: 36) draws a distinction between the 'Inspired Writer' and the 'Real Writer': the first 'is a figure for whom writing comes easily' whereas the second 'admit[s] to struggling with writing' (p. 35). Most child authors will fall into the second category and one of the reasons for this struggle is the need for inspiration to 'fire their desire' to put pen to paper/finger to keyboard. The ideas presented below are random in their content yet are deliberately inspirational in their drive to get child authors mark making/writing emerging stories.

Early Years Foundation Stage

- 'Set up the water tray with rotary whisks and a mild shampoo or bubble bath... challeng[e child authors] to create a bubble mountain for the "Bubble Beast" to live on' (Brownhill, 2009: 23). Invite them to mark make/write about the day that they go for a walk with their friends on the mountain and encounter the *Bubble Beast*. '*What happens when the Beast tries to capture you as his real-life teddy bears?*'
- Show child authors pictures/images of airport conveyor belts. Talk about how passengers are always keen to see their case after their flight. '*What would your suitcase look like? Think about its colour, size and shape.*' Get them to imagine that they open their case and are shocked when someone/something jumps out! Get them to mark make/write an emerging story about their suitcase surprise. *Is it a snake? A jack-in-the-box? A Minion? A kangaroo?* Create a simple paper flap to 'reveal' the surprise!

Key stage 1

- There is a phrase which suggests that we are 'drawn to what we dread'. Read *Little Mouse's Big Book of Fears* (Gravett, 2007), getting child authors to make a list of their own fears and phobias – think *heights*, *spiders*, *the dark*, *noise* and *feet* (see http://tinyurl.com/pmxx2 for others). Encourage them to think about ways in which a story character who suffers from one of these fears or phobias manages to overcome this though *bravery, determination, anger, resourcefulness* or *support from their friends and family.* Might writing a short story about this help child authors who have a fear or phobia of story writing (writing reluctance) to overcome this?
- Let child authors look at non-fiction picture books about tornadoes. Invite them to write an innovative story about the day they get sucked up into a tornado and are dropped into unusual world (think *The Wizard of Oz* as inspiration), the innovation being that the text on each page of their paper story book is presented on a spiral writing line so that readers have to keep rotating the book around in their hands to actually read it!

Gold star!

Want some cracking story writing ideas to inspire child authors with? Then consider downloading the PDF available at http://tinyurl.com/mug8old, exploring the wealth of creative writing activities offered within it. Adapt these in response to the needs and capabilities of the child authors that you work with, dipping into this resource for ideas to stimulate weekend work/homework, holiday tasks or writing challenges. Other suggestions and advice can be found at http://tinyurl.com/okdkkvm and http://tinyurl.com/ppva4nx.

Story writing 'pick and mix' 8

Here is an eighth collection of stimulating story writing ideas to engage child authors and enrich professional practices. As explained in 'Story writing "pick and mix" 1' (see p. 23) this assortment of ideas is not attributed to a particular age phase but is offered more as a selection of suggestions for professionals to choose from and adapt in response to the mark making/writing needs of their learners – *put an 'X' by any that you think you might try out!*

X

↓

Story knitting: Invite child authors to write an emerging story about an auntie/granny/ mummy who likes to knit 'on the move' (while walking/running/on the bus). *'What kinds of things does she knit and what happens to those who wear these knitted garments?'* Suggestions might include a balaclava for a puppy who becomes an early morning villain ('*Rob-A-Dog*'), booties for a newborn baby that make him dance, or a scarf for a female teacher whose voice changes into a man's when she wears it as a triple loop.

Story statements: Whitaker (n.d.) identifies 'selected teaching practices that are well recognized in the profession as being effective in helping students develop as writers'. Download the PDF from http://tinyurl.com/6t232cg, exploring how the statements both validate and suggest improvements to existing emerging story mark making/writing provision and practices in the setting/school as part of a team/staff meeting.

Story engagement: Promote the notion of readers being *actively engaged* in child authors' emerging written stories by weaving into the tale 'engagement features' e.g. the drawing of a doorbell that the character (and reader) presses (*BING BONG!*), questions directed *at* the reader (*What do you think she should do?*), or tissue paper that can be torn up and thrown like confetti at the end of the story when the newly-wed protagonists leave the church or other registered religious building.

Story gift: 'The gift that keeps on giving' is an old advertising slogan of uncertain origin which serves as the inspiration for this idea. Give child authors at Christmas, on their birthday or at the end of the academic year a paper book (self-made/purchased) made up of blank pages. Invite them to fill it with emerging stories and illustrations for personal enjoyment or to be shared with others.

Story rewards: Epstein (2014) suggests that '[p]erhaps one of the most important aspects of developing children's [mark making/] writing is to provide positive reinforcement for their efforts without regard to grammar and spelling errors'. Talk to child authors about the kinds of reinforcement that *they* would like to receive from professionals (within reason!), be they in the form of *verbal praise, stars, stamps, sweetie treats, certificates* or *'special' writing resources* such as *scented pens, shaped erasers* or *sparkly notebooks*. It's then just a case of stocking up!

Setting/school-wide stories: The Teacher Support Force (2011) argues that 'when strategies for teaching writing include [setting/] school-wide celebrations of children writing, magic happens and teaching the writing process becomes a community event.' Visit http://tinyurl. com/l2zrns3 for details about the *Spring Flower* [Writing] *Show*, embracing and applying the practice described to other school-wide events e.g. *One Book/World Book Day/Book Week* (emerging stories written in response to selected books/themes), *PTA Auctions* (of 'first edition' child authors' emerging stories) and *Talent Shows* (music, dance and drama inspired by child author's emerging stories).

Chapter 9

Openly stimulating the story!

The box!

Research conducted by OnePoll on behalf of the makers of Ribena Plus (2012) found that children enjoy playing with boxes instead of other toys, gadgets and games. The inspiration for this Idea is credited to Catherine Hetherington who put a box in the middle of a circle of children and got them to think of creative ways of using the box as a way of generating ideas for their emerging story writing. The suggestions below consider the inspirational potential of just two different kinds of cardboard box and merely offer *initial* creative questions to spark imaginations rather than present 'the definitive'!

Early Years Foundation Stage: Washing machine box

- A house – *What kind of house is it? A cottage? A yurt? A castle? Who lives there? A king? A mouse? A goblin? Who comes to visit and why?*
- A cave – *Who or what is hiding in the deep, dark cave? Why are they hiding? Who are they hiding from?*
- A shop – *What kind of shop is it? What does it sell? Sweets? Toys? Space equipment? Who comes to buy things? What happens when all of the products become 'sold out'?*
- A pirate ship – *Who is on the ship and where is it sailing to? Who do the crew fight on their journey and capture? How much treasure do they have stashed 'below deck'? What happens when the ship capsizes?*

See http://tinyurl.com/pmpsytk (p. 2) for an innovative 'chatterbox' to stimulate speech, language and communication – *perhaps this could be 'found' in the box?*

Key stage 1: Grocery box

- A snail shell – *What makes this snail visually distinctive to other snails? Where is the snail going? Who does she or he meet on the way? Who tries to eat the snail? Do they succeed?*
- A safe – *What is inside? Who does the safe belong to? Who wants to steal what is inside the safe and why? How is the safe opened? With codes? Finger print recognition? Keys?*

- An animal basket – *What sort of animal is it for? Is the animal a pet/sick/a stray/from the zoo? Why is the animal hiding in the corner of the box?*
- A baby's sports car – *What kind of car is it in terms of make and colour? How fast can it go? Where does the driver decide to 'race' to? Rio? The end of the street? America? Scotland?*

See http://tinyurl.com/q9lrseh to inspire child authors to write a story and make an associated story box for a child who is blind. Also see http://tinyurl.com/pm2h86u.

> ## Gold star!
>
> Consider offering child authors a range of other different kinds of boxes (real/images) to stimulate their emerging story mark making/writing e.g. *jewellery, shoe, first-aid, lunch, ring, picnic, bird, fuse, cake, watch, pencil, match, wicker, chocolate, tool, money, juice, music, storage* and *popcorn*. Visit http://tinyurl.com/lek7enj and click on the green Box Picture Gallery link to see the wonderful potential that a simple box can have in the artistic minds of children. *How can this potential be used to fuel child authors' emerging story writing?*

The tube!

Many parents/carers see tubes, particularly those made of cardboard, simply as disposable objects; many professionals (hopefully) see tubes as potential 'gold' for emerging story stimulation! Invite child authors to collect different kinds of tubes from home e.g. *paper towel, cling-film, foil, gift wrap* and *poster* (check whether you are able to use toilet roll tubes in the setting/classroom as there are hygiene issues associated with their potential/actual use). With a little imagination these tubes can really inspire child authors as they talk about them, handle them and write emerging stories about and on them!

Early Years Foundation Stage

- Binoculars – *Who do they belong to? Where are they being used? What can be seen through them? Wildlife? The stars? Aliens? What do users see that make them happy/scared/surprised/angry?*
- Micro/megaphone – *Who is holding it? A singer? A presenter? Mummy? What do they say/sing/shout? Are they heard by everyone? Why/not?*
- Kaleidoscope – *What different shapes/colours can be seen inside? Who argues over who gets to play with it first? What happens when the kaleidoscope gets broken?*
- Coin holder – *How much money is there inside? What different kinds of coin are held in the holder? What will/could the money be used to buy? Who tries to steal the holder? Why?*

Key stage 1

- Telescope – *Who is using it? A sailor? An astronomer? A mad scientist? What are they looking for? What do they actually see? Is it good or bad? Why?*
- Ear trumpet – *Who/what is struggling to hear? What do they hear/think that they hear? What do other story characters think the ear trumpet is? A funnel? A megaphone?*
- Trophy – *What is the trophy for? A special achievement? Recognition of effort? Who wins/receives it? Is everyone happy that the recipient won/received it? Who sets out to win back the trophy?*
- Baton – *Who does it belong to? A conductor/runner/policeperson/cheerleader? How do they use it and why? What magical thing happens when the baton is waved up and down three times?*

Gold star!

Develop child authors' general knowledge by helping them to recognise other kinds of tubes they may not necessarily be aware of e.g. *display, florescent lighting, hamster, pasta, concrete, vacuum, feeding, inner, tubes for sweets* and *tube slides.* Consider the potential of these tubes in helping to set up problems for characters in child authors' emerging stories when these tubes either break, get a puncture, get blocked, split or shatter! Think about the tubes representing a home for different characters (think *Teenage Mutant Hero/Ninja Turtles*) or different types of tunnels (see *Tunnel* by Browne, 2008). *What happens when characters pop out the other side of the 'tunnel'?*

The hat!

Village Hat Shop (2015) wisely states that 'hats matter' – when we think of *The Cat in the Hat* and *Noddy* it is easy to see what makes them such visually distinctive characters. Professionals can help child authors to appreciate how much 'hats matter', not only when thinking about the physical appearance of their characters but also about their 'potential' in relation to stimulating different elements of their emerging written stories such as plot.

Early Years Foundation Stage

- Challenge child authors to match a collection of hats to picture cards of different characters who are associated with them e.g. a *witch's* hat, a *king's* crown and a *swimmer's* cap. Mix up the hat cards, getting child authors to mark make/write an emerging story about a story character's *new* hat and why they want to wear it e.g. *the witch wears a swimmer's cap because she is going to the baths to teach her cat how to swim.* Read *Mrs Honey's Hat* (Adams, 2007) for inspiration!

- Get child authors to try on different hats from the setting's hat box. Encourage them to physically move about in the outdoor play area as the characters who usually wear them, mark making/writing an emerging story about why they are moving in this way e.g. jigging about (*jester's hat – trying to make someone laugh*), running (*policeperson's hat – chasing after a criminal*) or marching (*soldier's helmet – on parade*).

Key stage 1

- Suggest that child authors write a short story about a character whose new hat 'sings' whenever they wear it on their head (an adaptation of the Sorting Hat from *Harry Potter*). '*What can it sing? Does it have a good voice? Does the wearer like it? Do they do a duet together? What happens when others learn of the magical abilities of the hat – does the hat become an online media star?*' Visit http://tinyurl.com/kzcm88u for professional information about the 'Six Writing Hats' to support child authors and their story writing.
- Encourage child authors to write a fantasy story about a hat that magically changes colour in response to the mood of the character who wears it when different things happen to them during the day. '*Why does the hat turn red/blue/black/yellow/pink?*' Visit http://tinyurl.com/n53lqd for colour and mood 'matches' in relation to special rings that might feature in a child author's emerging story.

Gold star!

Give child authors the opportunity to become child *designers*, designing (and making, where appropriate) a new hat for a story character. Encourage them to be creative with the style, shape, size, colour(s), fabric(s) and the way in which the hat is worn, ensuring that their decisions reflect or accentuate the personality traits of the character. Use this practical designing (and making) experience as 'story fodder' for an emerging written tale about a hat-designing competition (local/national) that is won by none other than the child author themselves!

Fabric!

English and Broadhead (2004: 17) claim that '[c]reativity comes from owning ideas and from seeing possibilities'. Professionals can promote this by simply offering child authors a piece of plain fabric (white, cotton, 3 m × 1 m approx.). Support them in 'seeing possibilities' by playing around with the fabric and manipulating it into different shapes, objects and articles that can be 'owned' by child authors as key items to drive their emerging written stories forwards. Use the ideas overleaf as inspirational suggestion starters!

Early Years Foundation Stage

- *A cloak* – Who does it belong to? A wizard? Little *White* Riding Hood? A superhero? Who do they meet on their 'day off'? What happens when the cloak is taken off?
- *A catwalk* – What is being modelled on the catwalk today? Who is doing the modelling? Are they happy to be doing it? What happens when water gets spilt on the catwalk?
- *Swaddling clothes* – Whose baby is wrapped up? What is the baby's name? Does the baby stay awake in them?
- *The sea* – Is the sea calm/icy/stormy? Who is flying above/sailing on/swimming under the sea? Do the sea conditions change? What happens to the people/animals that are above/on/in/under the sea?

Key stage 1

- *A cloud* – Is it a small or large cloud? What does it float over? Why is it cheery/down/angry/moody/bored? What falls out of it when it 'rains'? Sherbet? Sprinkles? Fish? A UFO?
- *A tent* – What kind of tent is it? Where has the tent been put up? A field? A back garden? Who is in the tent and how many people can fit in it? Why has it been put up? A sleepover? An event? Shelter?
- *A sling* – Who has been hurt? How did it happen? Which body part is broken/sprained? An arm? Leg? Shoulder? Who is to blame? How long does it take to heal?
- *A bridal veil/train* – Who is getting married? To whom? Where is the wedding taking place – not a church? What is the theme of the wedding? Is everyone happy about the wedding?

Gold star!

Provide child authors with a range of different types of fabric that they can handle e.g. *silk, felt, mesh, lace, flannel, velvet, linen, wool, satin, gauze, leather, tweed, suede, corduroy, denim* and *faux fur*. Develop and extend vocabularies by getting child authors to describe these fabrics using a blindfold or a feely box, prompting them with new words (see http://tinyurl.com/k9xualw). Encourage child authors to use these adjectives to enrich written descriptions of their characters' clothing and other textured body parts e.g. *soft* skin, *stubbly* chin, *smooth* hands and *furry* legs! For younger child authors invite them to physically add these fabrics to their illustrations to create 'sensory sketches'!

The suitcase!

'The suitcase was old and battered and on the side, in large letters, were the words WANTED ON VOYAGE.' Any idea whose famous suitcase Bond (2008: 14) is describing? *That's right – Paddington Bear's!* With suitcases being of importance to

Abbie Rose (see Humphreys, 2013), child authors should be given the opportunity to explore the potential that suitcases might have for their own emerging stories!

Early Years Foundation Stage

- Use role play opportunities for child authors to 'play pack' a toy suitcase they would take on holiday to the seaside. Encourage them to draw/label these items on paper that has been shaped to represent an open suitcase. Support them in mark making/writing an emerging story about what they plan to do at the seaside. *'Do you want to build sandcastles? Eat ice cream? Paddle in the sea? What must you remember to pack to be able to do these things?'*
- *'Close your eyes and imagine that Teddy is having a sleepover at his friend's house tonight. What would he need to pack?'* Invite child authors to verbally share their own sleepover experiences to help identify necessary items. Get them to mark make/write an emerging story about an important item that Teddy forgets. *'What does he use as a substitute when he finds he has not packed his own teddy? How does he brush his fur when he realises he forgot to pack his body brush?'*

Key stage 1

- Present child authors with the following stimulating story title: *The Suitcase Challenge!* As a class, thought shower ways in which a suitcase could be used as part of a contest e.g. *seeing how many household items can fit into a small case, putting on as many clothes from a packed suitcase against the clock* or *weightlifting a heavy suitcase as many times in a minute as they can with one hand.* Encourage child authors to write a short story involving two characters who take up one of these suggested challenges. *Who is going to win, why and how?*
- Listen to *The Terrible Suitcase* (see http://tinyurl.com/psfjzwd). Use the teachers' notes – see http://tinyurl.com/m5nhzn4 – to stimulate active discussions and engaging story writing activity based around the suitcase as suggested by Holmes, particularly at the start of the school year (September).

Gold star!

Suitcases can be used to stimulate child authors' emerging story writing not only at school but also at home – see http://tinyurl.com/kvmp9w5 for a wonderful American-based family literacy project for young children that uses a *writing suitcase* (*writing rucksacks* and *weekend writing bags* serve as alternatives for those in KS1). This is a particularly useful idea for professionals who work with child authors in deprived areas. Alternatively promote the idea of *No Pen Wednesday* every day at home (see http://tinyurl.com/lc96xdp for information)!

Timepiece!

'*Hickory dickory dock, the mouse ran up the clock...*' Have you ever wondered what sort of clock it was? Illustrations that accompany this well-known nursery rhyme suggest that it was a grandfather clock. With a bit of imagination though it *could* be Big Ben, the famous clock in London or it *could* be a carriage clock with a baby/dwarf mouse! Child authors can use timepieces (examples of which are offered below) as a useful resource for stimulating their emerging stories as the following ideas so aptly suggest!

Mobile/smart phone	Desktop clock	Bedroom alarm clock	Pocket watch
Nurse's fob watch	Musical clock	Digital stop watch	Cuckoo clock
Kitchen wall clock	Wrist watch	Microwave clock	Water clock
Speaking clock	Hourglass	Oil lamp clock	Egg timer

Early Years Foundation Stage

- Encourage child authors to talk about things they like to do in the daytime when the sun is 'awake' and at night-time when the sun 'goes to sleep'. Invite child authors to mark make/write an emerging story about one of these activities, presenting their ideas on a paper clock face – see http://tinyurl.com/pxothda for a useful PDF.
- Develop child authors' understanding of the passing of time by getting them to consider different events which occur in their daily lives e.g. in the morning I '*brush my hair.*' In the afternoon I '*play with my toys.*' In the evening I '*have a bubbly bath!*' Other key words to promote include *yesterday, today, tomorrow, now, soon, before, after, next, last* and days of the week. Support child authors in using some of these words to mark make/write their emerging story about a 'silent day' using zig-zag folded paper.

Key stage 1

- Tell child authors the opening of a story called *The Bag of Clocks* in which a character stumbles across a *ticking* bag on the street. Upon looking inside the bag the character finds a collection of wind-up clocks, each one displaying a different time. As the character's iPod tells them that it is 12 o'clock the character decides to set all of the clocks to the right time. As the hands of the final clock both point to 12... '*Whatever happens next?*'
- Get child authors to imagine that they have been given a magical timepiece for their birthday (think Hermione's 'Time-Turner' in *Harry Potter and the Prisoner of Azkaban* – see http://tinyurl.com/b3bhkk) which allows them to travel back or forwards in time. '*Where do they go? Who do they meet? What do they see? What happens as a result of their time travel? How do they get back to "their time"?*'

Gold star!

Research carried out by YouGov for the education publishers Pearson (cited in Paton, 2012) revealed that one-in-six mothers and fathers admit that they never read to their children before bedtime. Encourage child authors to read/talk about *their* emerging written stories (be they initial ideas, 'work in progress' or the final draft) to their parents/carers before they go to sleep at night whenever possible in an effort to positively address this concerning statistic. Alternatively, get parents/carers and child authors to orally create stories together at bedtime to promote literacy and language development (see Cutspec, 2006).

The bottle!

'[Alice] went back to the table…this time she found a little bottle on it…round the neck of the bottle was a paper label, with the words "DRINK ME" beautifully printed on it in large letters.' Carroll (2008: 16) famously used the contents of the little bottle to help change the physical size of his well-known protagonist. Think about the story potential that the contents of different bottles could have in the creative minds of young child authors – *characters could grow wings, change colour, turn into stone, develop superpowers, speak 17 languages* or *become invisible.* Other exciting 'bottled' ideas that professionals can use to stimulate child authors' emerging story writing include:

Early Years Foundation Stage

*   Encourage child authors to play with a range of different bottles that are commonly found in the home environment e.g. *ketchup, shampoo, milk, sun cream, talc, washing-up liquid, soft drink/water* (ensure these are not made of glass and have been *thoroughly* washed out before being used). Support child authors in mark making/writing an emerging story that warns of funny things that could happen if characters mixed up the bottles e.g. *'Oh no! Sun cream on your toast!'* or *'Whoops! Shampoo on your sandwiches!'* (Remember – *don't try this at home!*)
*   Read *Pants* by Andreae and Sharratt (2003). Develop child authors' descriptive language by drawing/mark making/writing about different kinds of *bottles* – think *size, shape, colour, contents* – that can be collated into a collaborative bottle-shaped book or presented/labelled on a 3D display e.g. *'Tall ones, green ones, tiny little titchy ones…'*

Key stage 1

*   Encourage child authors to vary the contents of bottles that are found by characters in their picture-book stories so they do not always contain liquids or food. Contents could include *sand, coins, ribbons, animals, petals, model ships, pens, sawdust, miniature cars* or *paper shapes.* Get child authors to describe where characters find these bottles and what happens when they open them e.g. (animals):

'*Are the animals friendly or angry? Are they real or mythical animals? Do they become pets or escape and cause a lot of damage to people's houses? Why? How are they stopped?*'

- Read *Memory Bottles* (Shoshan, 2004). Suggest that child authors write a story based on a memory that they would like to preserve in one of Mr. McAllistair's bottles. '*What happened? Who was involved? When did it happen? Why is it memorable?*' Present this as a gift for a family member in the form of a *Story in a Bottle* (Brownhill, 2013: 63).

Gold star!

In the summers of 2013 and 2014 Coca-Cola replaced its iconic logo on its bottles with over 1,000 of the most popular names in Great Britain as part of its *Share a Coke with...* campaign. Invite child authors to take part in a setting/class/school *Share a story with...* campaign which involves them writing an emerging story, popping it into a recyclable plastic bottle and attaching a waterproof sticky label to its side on which is written '*Share a story with _____*' (enter the name of a different child author here). Put the bottled stories into a water tray (EYFS) or a paddling pool (KS1), select a bottle using a net, and find the child whose name matches the label, sharing the written emerging story with them.

String!

Children are known for asking some wonderful questions. Professionals are also known for giving wonderful answers in response to these! Take a look at this classic exchange between a child and their teacher:

Child: How long should my story be, Miss?
Teacher: It should be as long as a piece of string!

Professionals can use string as a versatile resource to stimulate and support child authors' emerging story mark making/writing in their settings/classrooms, practical ideas of which are offered below.

Early Years Foundation Stage

- Give child authors a small piece of string each, getting them to pretend it is a snake, a worm or a caterpillar. Suggest they physically take their animal on a little exploration around the setting. *Where do they go? What/who do they see?* Encourage them to mark make/write an emerging story about where they go, ensuring that they give a name to their animal!
- Develop child authors' speaking/listening skills and alphabetical ordering by suggesting they work with professionals to make up a short emerging story that makes reference to characters/settings/objects that begin with different letters of

the alphabet e.g. *'One sunny day Andy woke up and got out of bed. He had some coco pops and a drink...'* As each item appears in the story child authors could shape their piece of string into the corresponding letter (lower/upper case) as appropriate. Get them to mark make/write their favourite part of the story to share with others.

Key stage 1

- Ask child authors to create a physical outline of a Story Mountain with a piece of string (see http://tinyurl.com/ll72egt). On small pieces of paper encourage them to plan different parts of a 'bumped head' story, positioning these on their Mountain as appropriate. Suggest that they regularly refer to this as a 'direction tool' as they 'put the flesh on the bones' of their written story.
- Create verbal stories (which can be subsequently written down) by passing a ball of string *across* a small circle of child authors who each must contribute *the next sentence* to a story. Encourage child authors to keep hold of their part of the string to build a visual *story web*. Start different stories with the following: *It was only 7 o'clock when...; There was a loud scream from the kitchen...; Jamie opened the door to see the dustbin eating Grandma...; It had been snowing now for 11 straight days when all of a sudden...*

Gold star!

Storytellers such as Ruth Stotter and David Titus strongly advocate the use of string when telling stories. See pp. 3–45 of Pellowski's *The Story Vine* (available at http://tinyurl.com/mgqe6xs) which serves as 'a source book of unusual and easy-to-tell stories from around the world' (p. i) that use string. Model how to tell these stories in the setting/classroom by using and adapting Pellowski's guidance, challenging child authors to verbalise their own emerging written stories to parents/carers at home with string as part of their weekend work/homework activity.

The present!

Offer any child a wrapped present and professionals are likely to immediately engage their interest: *'I wonder what's inside?'* This curiosity can be captured in child authors' emerging stories if they are encouraged to write about gifts and the many activities associated with them e.g. *deciding what to get and how much to spend, the wrapping, the giving and receiving, the recipient's reaction* and *the subsequent use of the gift*. It is argued that there is nothing better than giving/receiving a story book as a present – *perhaps child authors might mark make/write one instead of having to always raid their piggy bank or ask their parents/carers to buy a gift!*

Early Years Foundation Stage

- Display a collection of wrapped presents. Allow them to handle <u>but not open them</u> – *can they guess what is inside?* Invite them to mark make/write an emerging story about what they think one of the gifts is, based on their investigations, imagining that it is one of their birthday presents. Open the gift. *How close were they to predicting the gift correctly?*
- Read *My Presents* (Campbell, 2015). Show child authors a selection of presents and a selection of loose name tags – tell them that Postman Pat took the presents out of his post sack and all the labels had come off! *Who do they think the presents belong to?* Get them to mark make/write an emerging story about a creative way that Pat works out who each of the presents is for e.g. *smelling it, feeling it, peeling a bit of the wrapping away, weighing in his hands* or *looking at its shape.*

Key stage 1

- Get child authors to talk about their (step)mummy or (step)daddy. '*What kinds of things do they like?*' Invite them to identify a great gift for (Step)Mother's Day/(Step)Father's Day. *Which shop could they buy it from? Why would their (step)mummy/(step)daddy like it? What could they do with it?* Encourage child authors to write a story about the above, only to find that another family member has bought them the same gift! '*Oh no! What are you going to do?*'
- Get child authors to draw pictures on whiteboards of items that they would <u>dislike</u> receiving as a gift e.g. *wellington boots, a bar of soap, a pillow cushion, a potato peeler* or *a packet of tissues.* Challenge child authors to write a short story in which they receive one of these gifts and how they react to it once the wrapping paper has been torn off it. What if they later find out that the gift was bought with all the money that the gift giver had available. *How do they feel now? Should they always be grateful for anything that they are given?*

Gold star!

It is suggested that dreams are a rich source of inspiration for writers – think Shakespeare's *A Midsummer Night's Dream* (Matthews, 2003). Encourage child authors to 'capture' dreams through conversations with peers and professionals, drawings, marks, key 'trigger' words and written sentences presented in clouds, stars, totem poles or dreamcatcher templates. Use these as the basis for an emerging fantasy story about dreams that come true, dreams that are stolen or adventures that they or their characters have that were 'just a dream'.

Story writing 'pick and mix' 9

Here is a ninth and penultimate collection of stimulating story writing ideas to engage child authors and enrich professional practices. As explained in 'Story writing "pick and mix" 1' (see p. 23) this assortment of ideas is not attributed to a particular age phase but is offered more as a selection of suggestions for professionals to choose from and adapt in response to the mark making/writing needs of their learners – *put an 'X' by any that you think you might try out!*

X

Story pill: Talk to child authors about an imaginary pill that when taken allows story characters to speak a foreign/strange language fluently and with understanding. *'Which language is their protagonist able to speak? French? Chinese? Welsh? 'Gobble-de-gook'? What happens when the effects of the pill wear off?'* Write this up as a comical emerging story.
Story magnets: Offer child authors a number of large sticky labels. Get them to draw a line down the centre of each label so that they represent the two poles of a bar magnet. Direct child authors to offer a story starter sentence on the *right* side of one of the 'magnets' (it could be about a pen pal, a fortune teller or a telephone call). Continue the written story on the *left* side of a *different* 'magnet', moving onto the *right* side of the same 'magnet' before continuing the story on the *left* side of a new 'magnet'. Mix up the 'magnets' and get peers to try and join the magnet ends together to create a coherent story on the floor, the wall or on a display board.
Story casts: Offer child authors recyclable tubes or boxes into which they can put different parts of their body that are 'broken' e.g. *legs* and *arms*. Get them to imagine that these cardboard resources represent plaster casts onto which child authors can mark make/write emerging stories to keep injured patients entertained as they wait for their bones to heal!
Story wrapping: Provide child authors with large sheets of paper onto which they can mark make/write their emerging stories of adventure, excitement and intrigue! Use this paper as wrapping paper for presents (birthday, Christmas or Eid) given to children by a setting/class professional. Extend this idea by creating *story* birthday/Christmas cards, ensuring there is space left for the receiver to enter their name into the relevant parts of the story to make it all about them!
Story toys: When it is 'Toy Friday' at the setting/school (the last day before half term or the holidays) encourage child authors to capture the stories that they make up with their toys and their friends on paper e.g. *What happens when Sindy and Barbie meet for the first time? Where does Doctor Who take Action Man as part of their 'Three Minute Madness Challenge' they set each other?* Alternatively, for those child authors and professionals who are interested in Lego, consider investing in a *Lego Education StoryStarter kit* (see http://tinyurl.com/q6nf3jq for more information)!
Silent story: Tell child authors an oral story but *do not* make any audible sound (tell them that the story can only be heard by dogs because your voice is pitched so high). Get child authors to carefully look at your facial expressions and your body movements. *Can they guess what the story is about?* Invite them to mark make/write their version of the story on paper. Retell your story, tweaking your ear as a 'frequency modulator' so that your child authors can now hear it. *How do the stories compare?*

Chapter 10

Getting started!

Tremendous titles!

Child authors can mark make/write the most wonderful emerging story that can be 'wrapped up' in a beautifully self-designed front cover, but if the story title does not grab the reader's attention then they [the reader] are unlikely to want to read it! Story titles such as *The Life Cycle of the Flea* and *Sammy's 29th Boring Day at the Bus Stop* just do not cut it; story titles should embrace the 3Cs rule: *catchy*, *concise* and *curious*. Share with child authors the suggested titles below to both exemplify the 3Cs rule and stimulate their emerging story mark making/writing.

Early Years Foundation Stage		
My wet weekend!	Poppy the dog is lost!	It's time for bed!
It's party time!	Finger fun!	Let's go to the park!
Who loves Mummy?	Who's in the den?	Harry's new hat!
Puddle play!	The best of friends!	My funny face!*

* Story titles do not necessarily need to have exclamation/question marks at the end of them.

Key stage 1		
Hide-a-way Hugo	Helping Dad out	Our upside-down day!
Down the drain we go!	The big ball in the tree	The Monster Disco
Follow my leader	The giggle jar	A breakfast fit for giants
Maypole madness!	Plaster cast!	The wishing well

Show child authors how to 'unpick the possibilities' of suggested story titles by modelling the process of thought showering *questions for consideration* <u>around</u> the title on an easel/IWB. For example:

How messy is Messy Max – just a little or really messy?	*What does Max physically look like? How old is he?*	*Could Max actually be a girl – Max<u>ine</u>?*
Does Max want to be part of the Spring Clean? Why / not? How does he try to avoid it? Does he succeed?	**Messy Max and the Spring Clean**	*What does Max have to spring clean? His bedroom? How do we [the reader] know that it needs to be spring cleaned?*
Is there anyone else involved in the Spring Clean e.g. Mum? Dad? Brothers and sisters?	*What specific month / day does the Spring Clean take place on? Is it important to know this?*	*Who asks / makes Max take part in the Spring Clean? What does Max find during the clean?*

Invite child authors to select story books from the book corner/box/library (setting/local)/their home collection or from online lists, sorting these, with support, into two book boxes, one for titles that they like and the other for those they dislike. Get them to explain *why* they like particular titles, noting down and displaying these reasons – these can be used as a useful aide-memoire of what makes a 'good' story title e.g. 'snappy', one-word titles (*Dogger*), alliterative titles (*Mrs Honey's Hat*), or those that use onomatopoeic words (*Whoosh and Chug!*). Alternatively, get child authors to generate engaging story titles using the *Story Title Ideas* generator at http://tinyurl. com/pntfbkj.

Note!

Maynard (2002: 99) found that children's difficulties in coming up with 'good ideas' for their story writing can actually stem from 'the...teachers' choice of story title'. Professionals should be encouraged to offer a *balance of provision*, letting child authors write with a 'free mind' so that they can use *their* 'good ideas' about *themselves* to maintain their 'enthusiasm' for emerging story mark making/writing.

Gold star!

Show child authors how to 'tweak' well-known children's story titles to create new ones which they can use as stimuli for their own emerging tales e.g.

Key stage	Well-known story title	'Tweaked' story title
EYFS	Goldilocks and the Three Bears	Goldilocks and the Three Little Pigs
	Owl Babies	Toddler Toucans
KS1	I Want My Hat Back	I Want My Pants Back
	The Rainbow Fish	The Kaleidoscope Koala

If older child authors struggle to initially decide on a 'cracking' emerging story title suggest they offer a temporary *working title* that can be changed once their

story is complete (think *Blue Harvest* for the film *Star Wars: Return of th*
Alternatively, they could give their emerging story a secretive title such as *Projeci*
H until it 'goes public' (is read by others).

A sentence starter for 10!

Moore (2005: 2) suggests that 'a lack of varied sentence starters [in children's writing is] a source of endless frustration in the writing process' – without this variety child authors' stories can become repetitive and dull: *And then...and...and...and...!* Professionals can stimulate child authors' emerging storytelling/mark making/writing by offering them/modelling a wealth of *sentence starters/stems/openings* to 'pick and choose' from, using the display strategies also advocated below:

Early Years Foundation Stage		Display strategies
• I/we go to...	• Can you see a/my...?	• On leaves (painted or real)
• He/she is...	• Here is a/my...	• On simple 'paper-strip' bracelets/chains
• I/we have...	• This is a/the/my...	
• I/we can...	• I like a/the/my...	• On lollipop sticks (coloured)
• I/we play...	• I like to go to...	• On modes of transport (2D or 3D e.g. car, boat, plane)
• I see/saw...	• Look at...	
• I was...	• Come to the...	• On footprints (painted)
• I look at...	• Go on the...	• On caterpillar 'body balls'
• Look at me in the...	• It is a...*	• On shiny CD faces
• Can you...?		

* Adapted from Kindergartenteacherclaire (2010).

Many of the sentence opener suggestions offered for KS1 below can be found in the document *Literacy Curricular Targets: Sentence Openers* which is available at: http://tinyurl.com/o9hfx6n. These relate to the VCOP features associated with Ros Wilson's *Big Writing* (see http://tinyurl.com/ocrentr for more information).

Key stage 1		Display strategies
• A...	• At last...	• On lily pads or stepping stones (painted)
• My...	• After a while...	
• The...	• Although...	• Inside open boxes
• First...	• Before...	• On coloured handprints
• Then...	• Afterwards...	• On individual 'patches' which make up the skin of *Elmer* the elephant
• Next...	• Eventually...	
• After that...	• Sometimes...	
• Finally...	• Often...	• On train tracks (in the gaps between the sleepers)
• Soon...	• Slowly...	
• Suddenly...	• Quietly...	• On paper clothing hung on a washing line

Other sentence starters can be found in *Progression in Language Structures* (Tower Hamlets EMA Team in collaboration with Tower Hamlets teachers, 2009). Further examples of sentence starters that professionals might use to extend more abled child authors include:

• Once...	• The last time...
• On...	• Late that night...
• They...	• From now on...
• During...	• Another time...
• So...	• As soon as...

Consider displaying these sentence starters (and others) on *paper plates, leaflets, the labels on empty bottles, stones (chalked on), old DVDs, badges (self-made), luggage tags, face towels (stitched on)* or *mugs (painted on)*.

Gold star!

Engage child authors in practical sentence-making games to stimulate and enrich their emerging story mark making/writing. Useful resources can be found at the following websites:

http://tinyurl.com/psn8f7z   http://tinyurl.com/y9fbb9p   http://tinyurl.com/axa4gkv

Alternatively, for those child authors who just need an opening sentence to 'get them off the writing blocks', visit http://tinyurl.com/yke6mh8 for 194,480+ choices that can be adapted and used for storytelling and emerging story mark making/writing!

Curiouser and curiouser!

Carroll's (2008) famous protagonist Alice, uttered the words which make up the title of this Idea. They seemingly serve as the inspiration for Babauta (2008) who suggests that to create a great beginning to a story authors need to '[g]et them [readers] curious. Beyond just getting their attention, you have to arouse their curiosity, so that you can hold their attention, and get them to want to read more. Be different.' Professionals should therefore encourage child authors to mark make/write emerging story openers that are purposefully intriguing and yet a little odd!

Early Years Foundation Stage

• Support child authors in making a Halloween mask (see http://tinyurl.com/qzb36ug for ideas). Once wearing them, get child authors to think about unusual sounds or made-up words that their Halloween character might make that scares those who hear/see them e.g. *'Blerbble!' 'Frrrrr!'* and *'Muh-hum-mur!'* Encourage child authors to mark make/write an emerging story about their character, translating what he/she/it was actually trying to say e.g. *'Be my friend!'*, *'Where is the toilet?'* or *'I'm so tired!'*

- Offer child authors some items of play clothing and get them to wear them inappropriately e.g. *upside down/back to front/inside out/worn on wrong parts of the body*. *'Why would someone dress like this?'* Get child authors to mark make/write an emerging story about a character who wears clothes in unusual ways because they want to make people laugh, they are having a 'silly' day or they are late for their session/school and so hurriedly got dressed.

Key stage 1

- Talk to child authors about exclamations which can be defined as a sudden cry or remark expressing surprise, strong emotion or pain. Get child authors to generate and use exclamatory sentences at the start of their written story set in the deep rainforest to fascinate the reader to get them to want to read on e.g. *'Your feet are* **gigantic!***'* (Whose feet were they?); *It was absolutely **revolting!*** (What was?); *We hurt **all** over!* (Why?).
- Visit http://tinyurl.com/mr4v9lk which offers the '100 best opening lines from children's books'. Get child authors to select one, modelling how it can be altered by changing nouns, verbs and adjectives to make a bizarre opener for their written fantasy story e.g. 'All children, except one, grow up' (*Peter Pan* – Barrie, 2010: 1) becomes 'All puddings, except two, are sweet and friendly'!

Gold star!

There are times when child authors should be encouraged to 'cheat' a little when mark making/writing their emerging stories – think Corbett's *Nick the Magpie* (see http://tinyurl.com/pz69uty)! This ***does not*** mean that they should deliberately plagiarise another author's work but instead should make use of professional-selected 'quick-fire' writing tips/guidance/strategies/advice offered on the *Cheat Sheets* available at http://tinyurl.com/2edpfrs and http://tinyurl.com/kfjbttf. Select and adapt these suggestions for the benefit of the child authors you work with, offering these in verbal and written form via teaching points, displays and summative comments.

Posing a question!

Stephen King (in Fassler, 2013) is adamant that '[a]n opening line should invite the reader to begin the story. It should say: Listen. Come in here. You want to know about this.' One way that this can be achieved is by posing a question to the reader. Child authors can use this not only as an interesting opening 'hook' to initiate their emerging story, but also as a way of assessing their 'attention grabbing' mark making/writing skills by observing readers reading their story (if possible) – if they *keep on* reading then their question was a success!

Early Years Foundation Stage

- During planned Talk Time opportunities invite child authors to answer simple verbal questions offered by professionals and peers e.g. *'What is your favourite colour? Who is your best friend? What do you like eating for breakfast?'* Encourage them to record their response to one of these questions through drawings/mark making/writing to create a separate page for a quizzically-titled cohort emerging story book e.g. *Who's Your Bestie* [best friend]*?*
- Encourage child authors to read/discuss simple stories that use questions for their title e.g. *Who's in the Shed?* (Parkes, 2001); *Where's My Sock?* (Dunbar, 2006) and *How Do You Feel?* (Browne, 2012). Suggest that child authors mark make/write their own short emerging story (with support) that is driven by a questioning title e.g. *'When is it time for bed? What's for tea? Why is Snoopy upset?'*

Key stage 1

- Many professionals use Bloom's Revised Taxonomy (Anderson and Krathwohl, 2001) as a planning tool to support them in determining and clarifying learning objectives and formulating questions. Visit http://tinyurl.com/8f6ksxc, adapting and displaying appropriate questions using child-friendly techniques (e.g. *on flowers/flags/buttons/question clouds/name cards*) so that child authors can use these as story openers e.g. *Where's Dermo* [the dog] *hiding? How much is Bunny? Who's making that racket* [noise]*?*
- Children naturally ask wonderful questions e.g. *Who invented clothes? Why doesn't Tarzan have a beard? How long is a piece of string? Why is the sky blue?* When these are asked 'capture' them in a class question book, challenging child authors to use one of these as an opener for their story e.g. *Does Bigfoot exist? Yes. He lives under my bed!* (Tommy, 5.9 yrs.) See Burningham (1994) for inspiration.

Gold star!

Role play areas have long been an effective and engaging feature of learning spaces for young children (EYFS). Cremin *et al.* (2008) strongly advocate the use of role play areas in KS1 classrooms to support quality learning and teaching. Work with child authors to create and enrich purposeful spaces for emerging story mark making/writing e.g. *The Writers' Room, Parable Publishers, The Authors' Atrium* or *The Story Shed* in which child authors can work-in-role *as* 'real' authors. See http://tinyurl.com/p8a6msh for information and some exciting ideas.

Sensory stimulation!

Many child authors will be familiar with Mr. Potato Head, the American toy that appeared as an animated character in the *Toy Story* films. A number of plastic parts which can be attached to his body represent the organs that allow us to see, smell, touch, taste and hear (*eyes, nose, hands (skin), mouth (tongue)* and *ears*). These senses play an essential role in our lives and can be used to stimulate and enrich child authors' emerging story mark making/writing – just see Slegers (2012)!

Early Years Foundation Stage

- Read *Brown Bear, Brown Bear, What Do You See?* (Martin, 1997). Use the repetitive sentence structure to help child authors offer their own ideas (through drawings and mark making/writing) as to what new animals in the story *see* e.g. *I see a 'pink rabbit...a cream zebra...a lilac rat' looking at me* (Brownhill, 2013: 91).
- Integrate *touch* into child authors' emerging stories by encouraging them to mark make/write an emerging story about a trip (real or imagined) to a farm or a petting zoo. '*What animals did you see? What did they feel like?*' e.g. 'There was a duckling. It was soft' (story dictation, Emily, 3.8 yrs). Enhance animal illustrations by helping child authors to select and attach materials to their accompanying drawings/paintings which have the tactile qualities of the animal's skin e.g. *faux fur, silk* and *leather.*

Key stage 1

- In *Peace at Last* (Murphy, 2007) Mr. Bear struggles to get to sleep because of all of the *sounds* he hears in different parts of the house. Help child authors to develop their understanding of onomatopoeic words by considering *other* noises that might keep them awake in their own house – *the* **squeak** *of the pet mouse; the* **ring-ring** *of the telephone* – writing a simple story about what prevents *them* as Mr _____ or Miss _____ from having a well-earned nap after a hard day at school. Also see the next Idea: 'Onomatopoeic "explosion"!' (p. 132).
- '*Think about your favourite food/drink – what do they taste like?*' Encourage child authors to enrich written descriptions of the food/drink characters consume to 'keep them going' in their stories of endurance (think *training for the sports day* or *writing an extended story!*) by using appropriate adjectives e.g. 'At half time Ben had some juice. It was cold and orangey. Ben liked it. He then ran fast and scored a goal against the Furious Fireworks football team' (Ben, 6.9 yrs). This also links well to the senses of *hunger* and *thirst.*

Gold star!

Engage child authors in practical activities that stimulate their senses using blindfolds, feely boxes, sound CDs, food samples and smelling pots (see http://tinyurl.com/lwxzzno for other ideas), drawing on these experiences to stimulate and enhance their emerging story mark making/writing. Explore the website http://tinyurl.com/nasojqc, inviting child authors to collaborate together to create a *multisensory* story which could be shared with children and adults in the local community who have learning difficulties.

Onomatopoeic 'explosion'!

It is said that if you want to grab the attention of your reader you should start your story off with a bang – that is exactly what Bethany Curtis-Christie did with her competition winning story entitled *Bang!* (Hawkinge Primary School, 2013). Whether they are used as a title (*Boom!*), the name of a story character (*Mr. Bump*) or as a sound effect (*SPLASH!*), onomatopoeic 'explosions' – words that imitate the sound they describe when pronounced – can be an effective way of both gaining and retaining child authors' readers! Exciting examples include:

Boom!	Thud!	Sssshblamm!	Dink!
Twang!	Dhummm!	Whizz!	Neee Narrr!
Pffffhhhhh!	Kapow!	Thump!	Ping!
Bosh!	Roar!	Plop!	Ssshhhwwwiiissshhh!
Wallop!	Slurp!	Kkkkhhhhh!	Crash!
Clatter!	Rarrrrr!	Ding Dong!	Splat!

Professionals might also promote the repetitive articulation of different phonemes as alternative sound 'explosions' (think *Jolly Phonics* – see http://tinyurl.com/o7l59dv). Encourage child authors to consider using these 'explosions' in their emerging stories through the use of the following ideas and suggestions:

Early Years Foundation Stage

- Challenge child authors to make explosive (*loud*) sounds with musical instruments in the outdoor play area, mimicking them with their voices and describing the sounds that they make. Create a group book entitled *The Noisy Hullaballoo* in which each child author contributes a page that contains a paper flap that hides a picture/photo of themselves playing an instrument. Support them in mark making/writing the onomatopoeic word(s) that describe the sound being made with the instrument repeatedly all over the page. *Can readers of the book guess who is making that noise? Why is everyone making such a lot of noise?*
- Get child authors to think of different animals who make onomatopoeic 'explosions' as they move about e.g. *elephants*, *giants*, *hippos* or *dinosaurs*. Support them in mark making/writing an emerging story that describes these different sounds e.g. *elfats gow bum bum bum wen va wc* ('Elephants go boom boom boom when they walk', Jessie, 5.7 yrs, independent writing).

Key stage 1

- Get child authors to imagine that they are going on an imaginary school trip to a farm, a park, a zoo or a fairground. Encourage them to thought shower all of the onomatopoeic 'explosions' they might hear during the trip, integrating these into their story about what happens during this exciting fictional outing that does not go quite to plan!

- In light of the fact that toilet humour is considered to be an initial stage in the development of humour in children (Kustermann, 2003 in Brownhill, 2013: 148), invite child authors to use 'naughty' onomatopoeic explosions in their silly stories to make readers giggle when characters are frightened, scared or get nervous about undertaking different things such as singing in front of the school or asking a girl/boy out e.g. *Pfurt! Parp! Ffffffff! Plop!*

Gold star!

Help child authors to develop a bank of useful onomatopoeic words by adapting the lyrics to the song *Old MacDonald* e.g. *And on that farm he had some <u>bells</u> ... with a <u>DING DONG</u> here...*; *And on that farm he had some <u>drinks</u>...with a <u>SLURP SLURP</u> here...* Alternatively, develop child authors' understanding and appreciation of onomatopoeia using comic books/strips or onomatopoeic pop art as a visual teaching resource.

Let me introduce myself!

Kendell (2004: 23) suggests that child authors can open a story by 'talk[ing] directly to the reader'. While Freeman (2010) finds this 'annoying', dialogue which is directed to the reader can be effective in both breaking down the 'fourth wall' (see http://tinyurl.com/l74ay4n for information) and attracting their attention so that they want to 'read on'. Support child authors in thinking about different ways of 'speaking' to readers that will intrigue and draw them into the emerging tale that they [child authors] want to tell/mark make/write.

Early Years Foundation Stage

- Many stories open with a question to make the reader think. Capture questions that child authors ask during a session in the setting, displaying these on an easel/IWB. During carpet time revisit these questions, getting child authors to consider one which would be good to start an emerging story with e.g. *Can I play? What's the time? Where are you going?* Encourage them to mark make/write an answer to the question for the reader e.g. *Yes! Snack time! To bed!*
- Support child authors in introducing themselves to their peers with the intent of making them giggle e.g. *'My name is Scott and I am smelly!' 'I'm Faye and I like big pants!'* Get child authors to mark make/write down these funny introductions, offering an amusing illustration which helps the reader to understand the fictitious 'truth' behind the humour e.g. *Scott is really a pig; Faye is a clown.*

Key stage 1

- Show child authors an empty jam jar. Get them to close their eyes and imagine that something (living) is trapped inside – think *a mouse, an alien, a spider* or *a fly.* '*What do you think the creature would say to you if you came across the jar while taking a walk in the park?'* (think the film *Ratatouille*). Use the character's verbalised sentence to open a lovely story about a friendship that blossoms from this 'chance finding'.

- Get child authors to think of things that story characters could do that are likely to shock the reader e.g. *they steal money; they walk through walls; they know the answer to every question in the world.* Suggest that child authors present one of these as the opening to an unbelievable story, directing this to the reader as a simple fact e.g. *I can walk through walls, you know! I have £1,000 under my bed! Jealous much?*

Gold star!

Effective professionals, like child authors, are like magpies that take good ideas and utilise them as part of their own practice. Enrich your adult-led provision/direct-taught input by using and adapting the suggested online story writing resources below:

EYFS	*Mark Making: Progression in Play for Babies and Children* (pp. 38–39)	http://tinyurl.com/k2mknfw
	Using StoryPhones to Support Reading and Writing in Reception and Key stage 1	http://tinyurl.com/or7t9om
KS1	KS1 Story writing ideas, prompts and story starters	http://tinyurl.com/oo22e3y
	Tell it Again! The Storytelling Handbook for Primary English Language Teachers	http://tinyurl.com/owdqbco

Lights! Camera! *Action!*

Professionals will recognise the title of this Idea as the traditional cue for a movie crew at the beginning of a 'take'. Pullman (2012: xiv) asserts that '[a] good tale moves like a dreamlike speed from event to event, pausing only to say as much as is needed'. With this in mind child authors should be encouraged to mark make/write emerging stories which incorporate lots of 'swiftness', not just to benefit the story plot (KS1) but also those who can be encouraged to be *physically active* when reading it (EYFS).

Early Years Foundation Stage

- Engage child authors in 'Total Physical Response games such as *Simon Says* and songs like *Head, Shoulders, Knees and Toes*' (Jones, 2012: 1). Build on this by teaching them simple stories that they can hear and act out – see http://tinyurl.com/pf4chhc, pp. 2–3. Encourage child authors to mark make/write one of these stories as an emerging retelling with support.
- Berkowitz (2011: 37) asserts that: '[W]hen children engage in a series of actions with purpose and direction, their physical experience can help them remember a story and its sequence better.' Get child authors to think of new things which

could scare the *Little Old Lady* [or Little Old Man] *Who Was Not Afraid of Anything* (Williams, 1986) – Lions? Chameleons? Hamsters? – considering suitable actions to accompany their emerging presence. Mark make/write an emerging story about the Little Old Lady's/Little Old Man's bravery as they try to get home on a dark and creepy night, sharing this with parents/carers.

Key stage 1

- Child authors will find it easy to write action stories if they are given or select a story theme which lends itself to 'action'. Model this with reference to 'A day at the beach' – think *tiptoeing on the hot sand* or *jumping over the waves* – integrating these into a shared/guided emerging story writing opportunity. Other action story themes include a rocket journey, a rollercoaster ride, the stormy night, being shipwrecked, 'scarecrow, magic carpet ride, visit to a farm, the zoo, a scary night, pirates, buried treasure, under the sea and walking through the [forest]' (NSW Health, 2009: 16).
- Engage child authors in a thrilling Rhino Chase (see http://tinyurl.com/ojjx29t for details). Get them to use this as the basis of an action story that captures the excitement and fear of their encounter with 'the beast'! Get them to 'relive' their experiences by writing the story down *really quickly*, having a rest and then looking back at it, making improvements to their spellings and sentences. Consider referring to Disney's *The Lion King* film for inspiration.

Gold star!

While busy professionals are understandably more interested in the WHAT and HOW of story writing it is important to sometimes consider the WHY of story writing (child authors also need to know this as they progress in their abilities). Read 'Vygotsky and the teaching of writing' (Everson, 1991), reflecting critically on the content of the article as part of your IPD/CPD. *How is the narrative practice in* your *setting/classroom underpinned by theoretical understanding?* Alternatively, see http://tinyurl.com/msovlsk for a wealth of writing stories resources to support the HOW of story writing in settings/classrooms.

Get the picture!

Cleese (2014: 140) asserts that any young writer should 'steal an idea that you know is good, and try to reproduce it in a setting that you know and understand'. While the idea of actively encouraging child authors to directly plagiarise others' work is *strongly* discouraged in this book (see p. 129), a dedicated attempt has been made below to creatively *adapt* a wealth of interesting ideas to stimulate children's emerging story writing. The title of this Idea mirrors that of the 1990s' Nickelodeon children's game show *Get The Picture*; the activities described are 'tweaked' from the games that were played during this engaging American programme.

Early Years Foundation Stage

- *You Draw It:* Get a child author to draw a picture of a simple single item/object on a whiteboard/easel while their peers try to guess what is being drawn (think *Pictionary*). The peer who successfully identifies the item/object should be then encouraged to use this as the basis of a simple emerging story that is verbally constructed with support from professionals and then committed to paper e.g. a butterfly serves as the inspiration for *The Flutterby Races*!
- *On the lookout:* Give child authors a pair of binoculars (real/play/made). Encourage them to scan the setting, identifying items of interest that story characters might decide to look for in a miniature search helicopter e.g. *jewels*, *lost pets*, *building bricks* or *people*. Get them to mark make/write an emerging story about what was found on the windy/snowy/rainy/sunny/cloudy day when they rode in the helicopter.

Key stage 1

- *Simon's* Photo Album:* Give child authors a selection of pictures/images of different characters and objects that are presented on a blank background. Get them to guess where these characters/objects might be found, justifying their reasoning with reference to published story books, posters and internet images. Challenge child authors to integrate their given characters and objects in a short written story, providing rich descriptions of their chosen setting to 'fill in the blankness' in the form of words and illustrations.
- *Simon's* Maze:* Give child authors an outline of a maze (see http://tinyurl. com/6hhtf26). Encourage them to initially work out how to navigate their way through the maze with a light pencil line. Then invite them to write a 'gathering-up' story that describes all of the different things that they collect as they work their way through the 'themed maze' – think Pac-Man – e.g. a *sweet/gold coin/ treasure/sports/musical instrument maze* – presenting the text along the navigation line! *'Who do characters give the items to when they manage to exit the maze? A local charity? Orphans? Those who are disabled or with learning difficulties?'*

* Other names are of course available!

Gold star!

Famous authors such as Michael Morpurgo, Margaret Atwood, Philip Pullman, Roddy Doyle and P.D. James were asked to list their ten rules for writing fiction as inspired by Leonard's (2010) *10 Rules of Writing*. Visit http://tinyurl.com/ kvjlxjq and http://tinyurl.com/nrlwm7o, identifying which of the 230+ rules presented you would adapt/share/advocate with your child authors to practically support their emerging story writing development. Encourage older child authors to formulate their own rules of writing, comparing these to those offered by 'the experts'.

Story writing 'pick and mix' 10

Here is the tenth and final collection of stimulating story writing ideas to engage child authors and enrich professional practices. As explained in 'Story writing "pick and mix" 1' (see p. 23) this assortment of ideas is not attributed to a particular age phase but is offered more as a selection of suggestions for professionals to choose from and adapt in response to the mark making/writing needs of their child authors – *put an 'X' by any that you think you might try out!*

X
↓

Story wind down: Ask child authors to imagine that you are a battery-powered storytelling robot. Start telling them an oral made-up story when – *Oh no!* – your batteries suddenly run out of power: *'...and...then......the.........monster...........!'* Get individual child authors to carry on the oral telling of the story; as they run out of ideas get them to slow down *their* speech, letting someone else pick up the story. Suggest that they mark make/write this up as a short emerging story for others to enjoy.
Story squirts: Provide child authors with large pipettes, empty Jif plastic lemon containers or water guns that can be used to mark make/write water-based emerging stories on the walls and floor of the outdoor play area, titles of which might include *Under the Sea, Bath Time* or *Learning to Swim*. Consider purchasing water-based food colouring to help distinguish between the text (one colour) and illustrations (another colour) that child authors create.
Story strokes: Handwriting Without Tears (n.d.) argue that: [w]hen [professionals] think it's time to help a child write letters, start with capitals. Capitals are the easiest letters to write, the easiest to recognize. They all are the same height and they all start at the same place (the TOP). Offer child authors various mark making materials that they can use to make straight line strokes with e.g. *brushes, sticks, chalks, finger paints* and *crayons*, joining individual lines together to form recognisable capital letters – think *A, E, F, H, I, K, L, M, N, T, V, W, X, Y* and *Z* to represent story text.
Hide and find stories: Get child authors to hide their written emerging stories around the setting (indoors and outdoors), challenging them to 'seek out' a story from another child author to read and enjoy! Older child authors could create a 'clue trail' to find the story or a story treasure hunt by offering clues to the next section of the story that have to be pieced together to create the 'full tale'.
Story occasions: Work with child authors to write types of stories for different occasions e.g. *Pillow stories* (emerging stories for bedtime), *Duvet Day stories* (emerging stories to chill out to) and *Scrub-a-dub-dub stories* (emerging stories for bath time). What kinds of stories could they write for *Wedding day, Birthday, Christmas Day* or emotional days e.g. *Happy day, Depressing day, Angry day* or *Exciting day?*
Story BANG! Support child authors in writing an emerging story in which there is a large **BANG!** e.g. *someone slamming a door, party poppers going off* or *things being dropped onto a roof/table/floor*. Visit http://tinyurl.com/p3vuo9c which provides instructions in helping child authors to make an origami banger to add some definitive 'audio' to their emerging story!

Conclusion

...tap-tap-tap.

The tapping finally stopped.

The end.

References

Adams, P. (2007) *Mrs Honey's Hat*. Swindon: Child's Play (International) Ltd.

Ahlberg, A. and Alhberg, J. (1999) *The Jolly Postman*. London: Puffin Books.

Alborough, J. (2004) *Where's My Teddy?* London: Walker Books.

Album, J. (2013) *Bea Gives Up Her Dummy*. Location unknown: Little Boo Publishing.

Allan, T. (2008) *The Mythic Bestiary: The Illustrated Guide to the World's Most Fantastical Creatures*. London: Duncan Baird Publishers.

Allen, S. (2010) *The Inspired Writer vs. the Real Writer*. [Online.] Available at: www.parlorpress. com/pdf/allen--the-inspired-writing-vs-the-real-writer.pdf (accessed: 18 January 2015).

Altman, H. (2010) Celebrity culture: Are Americans too focused on celebrities? In *Issues for Debate in Sociology. Selections From CQ Researcher*. [Online.] Available at: www.sagepub. com/upm-data/31937_1.pdf (accessed: 2 June 2015).

Andersen, H.C. (2014) *The Little Mermaid*. Location unknown: Hythloday Press.

Anderson, E.N. (2005) *Everyone Eats: Understanding Food and Culture*. New York: New York University Press.

Anderson, L.W. and Krathwohl, D.R. (2001) *A Taxonomy for Learning, Teaching and Assessing: A Revision of Bloom's Taxonomy of Educational Objectives*. Boston, MA: Allyn and Bacon.

Andreae, G. and Sharratt, N. (2003) *Pants*. London: Picture Corgi Books.

Appelcline, K. (n.d.) Writing dynamic settings. *Skotos*. [Online.] Available at: www.skotos.net/ articles/DynamicSettings.html (accessed: 7 December 2014).

Archer, J. (2014) *A Twist In The Tale*. London: Pan Books.

Armes, J. (2009) Teacher tips: Stimulate creative writing ideas with pictures. *EzineArticles*, 10 September. [Online.] Available at: http://ezinearticles.com/?Teacher-Tips---Stimulate-Creative-Writing-Ideas-With-Pictures&id=2904575 (accessed: 7 April 2014).

Armitage, R. and Armitage, D. (2007) *The Lighthouse Keeper's Lunch*. London: Scholastic.

Babauta, L. (2008) Short stories: The art of the start. *Write To Done*. [Online.] Available at: http://writetodone.com/short-stories-the-art-of-the-start/(accessed: 12 January 2015).

Balance Publishing Company (1989) *Read-Along Radio Dramas*. [Online.] Available at: www.balancepublishing.com/literary%20terms.pdf (accessed: 24 December 2014).

Baldwin, C. (2008) *Teaching the Story: Fiction Writing in Grades 4–8*, 2nd edition. Gainsville, FL: Maupin House Publishing Inc.

Barrie, J.M. (2010) *Peter Pan*. London: Puffin Books.

Baudet, S. (2013) No conflict – no story: Creating conflict in childrens books. *LiveGuru*. [Online.] Available at: http://live.guru/articles/no-conflict-no-story-creating-conflict-in-childrens-books (accessed: 2 April 2014).

BBC (2009) *My Story. Everyone Has a Story to Tell. What's Yours? Resources: Planning Your Writing*. [Online.] Available at: https://centreforfoundationallearning.files.wordpress.com/ 2012/09/mystory_planning.doc (accessed: 2 June 2015).

Beaty, A. (2013) *Rosie Revere, Engineer*. New York: Abrams Books for Young Readers.

Becta (2003) *What the Research Says about Using ICT in English*. Coventry: British Educational Communications and Technology Agency. [Online.] Available at: http://bee-it.co.uk/Guidance%20Docs/Becta%20Files/Reports%20and%20publications/Archive/04p%20wtrs_english.pdf (accessed: 11 June 2015).

Bell, J.S. (2004) *Plot and Structure: Techniques and Exercises for Crafting a Plot That Grips Readers from Start to Finish*. Cincinnati, OH: Writer's Digest Books.

Belot, M., James, J. and Nolen, P. (2014) *Incentives and Children's Dietary Choices: A Field Experiment in Primary Schools*. [Online.] Available at: www.bath.ac.uk/economics/research/working-papers/2014-papers/25-14.pdf (accessed: 1 February 2015).

Bennett, C. (2014) *Dough Disco Parent Workshop*. [Online.] Available at: www.hodgehillprimary.bham.sch.uk/pdfs/pres-doughdisco.pdf (accessed: 16 February 2015).

Berkowitz, D. (2011) Oral storytelling: Building community through dialogue, engagement, and problem solving. *Young Children*, March, 36–40. [Online.] Available at: www.naeyc.org/tyc/files/tyc/file/V5I2/Oral%20Storytelling.pdf (accessed: 3 April 2015).

Berkun, S. (2005) *#44 – How to Learn From Your Mistakes*. [Online.] Available at: http://scottberkun.com/essays/44-how-to-learn-from-your-mistakes/ (accessed: 12 June 2013).

Bernays, A. and Painter, P. (1990) *What If...? Writing Exercises for Fiction Writers*. New York: HarperCollins Publishers.

Bevan, C. (2007) What if? *Child Education Plus*, December. [Online.] Available at: http://images.scholastic.co.uk/assets/a/2c/94/story-starters-100615.pdf (accessed: 22 December 2014).

BFI (2003) *Look Again! A Teaching Guide to Using Film and Television with Three- to Eleven-Year Olds*. London: *bfi* Education. [Online.] Available at: www.bfi.org.uk/sites/bfi.org.uk/files/downloads/bfi-education-look-again-teaching-guide-to-film-and-tv-2013-03.pdf (accessed: 16 January 2015).

BFI (2004) *Starting Stories. Short Films for Three- to Seven-Year-Olds* (DVD). London: *bfi* Education.

BFI (2007) *Starting Stories 2. Using Short Stories in the Early Years, 3+* (DVD). London: *bfi* Education.

Blake, Q. (1999) *Mrs Armitage on Wheels*. London: Red Fox.

Blake, Q. (2000) *Mrs Armitage and the Big Wave*. London: Red Fox.

Blyton, E. (2008) *The Famous Five's Survival Guide*. London: Hodder Children's Books.

Bodenhafer, W.B. (1930) Cooley's theories of competition and conflict. *Publications of the American Sociological Association*, 25: 18–24.

Bond, M. (2003) *A Bear Called Paddington*. London: HarperCollins Children's Books.

Boryga, A. (2011) From one young writer to another: Creating human characters, Part 1 of 5. *Lit Drift*. 12 January. [Online.] Available at: www.litdrift.com/2011/01/12/from-one-young-writer-to-another-creating-human-characters-part-1-of-5/ (accessed: 28 December 2013).

Bowkett, S. (2010) *Developing Literacy and Creative Writing Through Storymaking: Story Strands for 7–12 Year Olds*. Maidenhead: Open University Press.

Braund, H. and Gibbon, D. (2010) *Funny Stories for Ages 5–7*. London: Scholastic.

Brown Agins, D. (2006) *Maya Angelou. 'Diversity makes for a rich tapestry.'* Berkeley Heights, NJ: Enslow Publishers.

Browne, A. (2008) *Tunnel*. London: Walker Books.

Browne, A. (2012) *How Do You Feel?* London: Walker Books.

Browne, E. (2006) *Handa's Surprise*. London: Walker Books.

Brownhill, S. (2009) *100 Ideas for Teaching Physical Development*. London: Continuum.

Brownhill, S. (2013) *Getting Children Writing: Story Ideas for Children Aged 3–11*. London: Sage.

Brownhill, S. (2014) Supporting teachers' reflective practice through the use of self-reflective shapes. *Pedagogical Dialogue*, 4(10): 132–135.

Brownhill, S. (2016) *Stimulating Story Writing! Inspiring Children in the 7–11 Classroom*. Abingdon: Routledge.

Browning, L. (n.d.) *What Do You Mean 'Think Before I Act?' Conflict Resolution With Choices*. A Teacher Inquiry Project. Submitted as Partial Fulfillment of the Requirements For the Degree Master of Education. Southwest Texas State University, San Marcos, Texas. [Online.] Available at: www.positivediscipline.com/research/What%20Do%20You%20Mean%20Think%20Before%20I%20Act.pdf (accessed: 20 April 2014).

Bullard, L. (2007) *You Can Write A Story! A Story-Writing Recipe for Kids*. Minnetonka, MN: Two-Can Publishing.

Burke, C.L. and Copenhaver, J.G. (2004) Animals as people in children's literature. *Language Arts*, 81(3): 205–213.

Burningham, J. (1994) *Would You Rather?* London: Red Fox.

Burningham, J. (2000) *The Shopping Basket*. London: Red Fox Books.

Butterworth, N. (2006) *Tiger in the Snow*. London: HarperCollins Children's Books.

Cairney, T. (2009) Key themes in children's literature: Problem solving. *Literacy, Families and Learning*, 14 May. [Online.] Available at: http://trevorcairney.blogspot.co.uk/2009/05/key-themes-in-childrens-literature.html (accessed: 17 January 2015).

Calderdale & Huddersfield NHS [National Health Service] Trust (2012) *The Narrative Activity Pack*. [Online.] Available at: http://tinyurl.com/loq4rt3 (accessed: 26 December 2014).

Campbell, R. (2010) *Dear Zoo*. London: Macmillan Children's Books.

Campbell, R. (2015) *My Presents*. London: Macmillan Children's Books.

Campbell, T.A. and Hlusek, M. (2009) Storytelling and story writing: 'Using a different kind of pencil'. *Research Monograph # 20, What Works? Research into Practice*, The Literacy and Numeracy Secretariat. Toronto: Ontario Ministry of Education.

Cantador, I. and Conde, J.M. (2010) Effects of competition in education: A case study in an e-learning environment. In *Proceedings of IADIS International Conference e-Learning 2010 (E-Learning 2010)* (July). Freiburg. [Online.] Available at: http://arantxa.ii.uam.es/~cantador/doc/2010/elearning10.pdf (accessed: 1 February 2015).

Carroll, L. (2008) *Alice's Adventures in Wonderland*. Eire: Evertype.

Carter, J. (2012) *Just Imagine: Music, Images and Text to Inspire Creative Writing*, 2nd edition. Abingdon: Routledge.

Carver, J.A. (2005) *4. Creating Human Characters*. [Online.] Available at: www.writesf.com/04_Lesson_01_Human.html (accessed: 28 December 2013).

Chen, C.-F.E. (2014) Folktales (or fairy tales). *Children's Literature*. [Online.] Available at: www2.nkfust.edu.tw/~emchen/CLit/folk_lit_type_folktale.htm (accessed: 7 January 2015).

Church, E.B. (2014) Why colors and shapes matter. *Little Scholastic*. [Online.] Available at: www.scholastic.com/browse/article.jsp?id=3746476 (accessed: 26 July 2014).

Clark, C. (2011) Setting the baseline: The National Literacy Trust's first annual survey into reading – 2010. London: National Literacy Trust. In DfE (2012) *Research Evidence on Reading for Pleasure*. [Online.] Available at: https://www.gov.uk/government/publications/research-evidence-on-reading-for-pleasure (accessed: 2 June 2015).

Clarke, J. and Featherstone, S. (2008) *Young Boys & Their Writing*. Lutterworth: Featherstone Education Ltd.

Cleaver, P. (2006) *Ideas for Children's Writers: A Comprehensive Resource Book of Plots, Themes, Genres, Lists, What's Hot & What's Not*. Oxford: How To Books Ltd.

Cleese, J. (2014) *So, Anyway…* London: Random House Books.

Coleman, P.T., Deutsch, M. and Marcus, E.C. (2014) *The Handbook of Conflict Resolution*, 3rd edition. San Francisco, CA: Jossey Bass.

Corbett, P. (2003) *How to Teach Story Writing at Key Stage 1*. London: David Fulton Publishers [reprinted 2010 by Routledge, Abingdon].

Corbett, P. (2006) *Story Telling into Writing*. [Online.] Available at: http://webfronter.com/lewisham/primarycommunity/other/Pie%20Corbett_Story%20telling%20into%20Writing%20220906.pdf (accessed: 8 September 2014).

Corbett, P. (2008a) *Storyteller: Traditional Stories to Read, Tell and Write*. London: Scholastic.

Corbett, P. (2008b) *The National Strategies – Primary: 'Storytelling' by Pie Corbett*. [Online.] Available at: www.foundationyears.org.uk/files/2011/10/Story-Teling_Story-Making1.pdf (accessed: 11 March 2014).

Corbett, P. (2008c) Warning stories. *Times Educational Supplement*, 12 May. [Online.] Available at: www.tes.co.uk/article.aspx?storycode=2345072 (accessed: 20 April 2014).

Corbett, P. (2015) *How to Teach Story Writing Ages 4–7*. London: David Fulton.

Cottringer, W.S. (2005) *Rectifying Mistakes*. [Online.] Available at: www.excellenceessentials.com/en/topleaders/all_articles/rectifying-mistakes_chnmsch4.html (accessed: 12 June 2013).

Cousins, L. (2013) *Noah's Ark*. London: Walker Books.

Cowley, J. (1998) *Do Not Open This Book!* Bothell, WA: The Wright Group.

Creffield, F. (n.d.) *Conflict Resolution: A Compromise for 5 Relationship Dilemmas*. [Online.] Available at: http://tinyurl.com/paqtpc7 (accessed: 31 December 2014).

Cremin, T. (2006) Creativity, uncertainty and discomfort: Teachers as writers. *Cambridge Journal of Education*, 36(3): 415–433.

Cremin, T. (2010) Motivating children to write with purpose and passion. In P. Goodwin (ed.) *The Literate Classroom*, 3rd edition. Abingdon: Routledge.

Cremin, T., Goouch, K., Blakemore, L., Goff, E. and Macdonald, R. (2006) Connecting drama and writing: Seizing the moment to write. *Research in Drama in Education*, 11(3): 273–291. [Online.] Available at: http://oro.open.ac.uk/9778/1/9778.pdf (accessed: 26 April 2014).

Cremin, T., McDonald, R., Goff, E. and Blakemore, L. (2008) *Jumpstart Drama!* London: David Fulton.

Cunha, D. (2013) Compromise activities for children. *Livestrong.com*, 7 March. [Online.] Available at: www.livestrong.com/article/562082-compromise-activities-for-children/ (accessed: 31 December 2014).

Cutspec, P.A. (2006) Oral storytelling within the context of the parent–child relationship. *Talaris Research Institute*, 1(2): 1–8. [Online.] Available at: www.talaris.org/wp-content/uploads/oralstorytelling.pdf (accessed: 2 April 2015).

Daily Mail (2012) Board game dads who hate to lose: Study finds fathers will go all out to win – but mothers are happy to see their children take victory. *Daily Mail*, 12 December. [Online.] Available at: www.dailymail.co.uk/news/article-2247310/Board-game-dads-hate-lose-Study-finds-fathers-win--mothers-happy-children-victory.html#ixzz305BJg5MQ (accessed: 27 April 2014).

Dargin, P. (1996) *Story Adaptation*. [Online.] Available at: www.australianstorytelling.org.au/storytelling-articles/n-s/story-adaptation-peter-dargin (accessed: 11 March 2014).

Daywalt, D. (2013) *The Day the Crayons Quit*. London: HarperCollins Children's Books.

De Haan, L. and Nijland, S. (2004) *King and King and Family*. Berkeley, CA: Tricycle Press.

DeNora, T. (2000) *Music in Everyday Life*. Cambridge: Cambridge University Press.

Despeaux, C. (2012) How to use misfortune to make your writing stronger. *OneWildWord.com*, 4 January. [Online.] Available at: http://onewildword.com/2012/01/04/how-to-use-misfortune-to-make-your-writing-stronger/ (accessed: 2 January 2015).

DfE (2011) *Almost 9 Out of 10 Parents Think Children Are Being Forced to Grow Up Too Quickly*. 11 April. [Online.] Available at: https://www.gov.uk/government/news/almost-9-out-of-10-parents-think-children-are-being-forced-to-grow-up-too-quickly (accessed: 27 February 2015).

DfE (2012) *What Is the Research Evidence on Writing? Research Report DFE-RR238*. [Online.] Available at: https://www.gov.uk/government/uploads/system/uploads/attachment_data/file/183399/DFE-RR238.pdf (accessed: 4 April 2015).

DfE (2013) *English Programmes of Study: Key Stages 1 and 2 – National Curriculum in England*. [Online.] Available at: https://www.gov.uk/government/uploads/system/uploads/attachment_data/file/335186/PRIMARY_national_curriculum_-_English_220714.pdf (accessed: 4 April 2015).

DfE (2014) *Statistical First Release: Early Years Foundation Stage Profile Results in England, 2013/14*. [Online.] Available at: https://www.gov.uk/government/uploads/system/uploads/attachment_data/file/364021/SFR39_2014_Text.pdf (accessed: 4 April 2015).

DfEE (1998) *The National Literacy Strategy: Framework for Teaching*. London: DfEE.

DfES (2001) *Stories With Familiar Settings – Aspects of Narrative, The National Literacy Strategy*. [Online.] Available at: http://tinyurl.com/qh7olk3 (accessed: 12 April 2014).

DfES (2003) *Excellence and Enjoyment: A Primary Strategy for Schools*. Nottingham: DfES.

Donaldson, J. (1999) *The Gruffalo*. London: Macmillan Children's Books.

Drachman, E. (2003) *Leo the Lightning Bug*. Venice, CA: Kidwick Books.

Duffy, C.A. (2007) *The Tear Thief*. Cambridge, MA: Barefoot Books.

Dunbar, J. (2006) *Where's My Sock?* New York: The Chicken House.

Durand, P. (2007) *The Quest Plot: How to Create a Quest Plot for Your Story*. [Online.] Available at: http://tinyurl.com/nftdpmv (accessed: 5 June 2015).

Early Education (2012) *Development Matters in the Early Years Foundation Stage (EYFS)*. [Online.] Available at: www.foundationyears.org.uk/wp-content/uploads/2012/03/Development-Matters-FINAL-PRINT-AMENDED.pdf (accessed: 4 April 2015).

Elks, E. and McLachlan, H. (2014) *Colourful Stories*. [Online.] Available at: https://elklantraining.worldsecuresystems.com/resources/colourful-stories (accessed: 8 June 2015).

Emery, D.W. (1996) Helping readers comprehend stories from the characters' perspectives. *The Reading Teacher*, 49(7): 534–541.

Emery, I. (2012) *A Crash Course in Flash Fiction*. [Online.] Available at: http://uca.edu/writingcenter/files/2012/06/Flash-Fiction.pdf (accessed: 25 February 2015).

Emmett, J. (2010) *Foxes in the Snow*. London: Macmillan Children's Books.

English, C. and Broadhead, P. (2004) Theatre and open-ended play in the early years – combining to promote opportunities for creativity. *Topic*, 32: 13–18. [Online.] Available at: www.nfer.ac.uk/nfer/pre_pdf_files/04_32_02.pdf (accessed: 12 June 2015).

Epstein, P. (2014) How to develop writing in young children. *eHow*. Formerly available at: www.ehow.com/how_7348833_develop-writing-young-children.html (accessed: 16 October 2014).

Evans, B. (2011) Bullying: Can it begin in preschool? *Extensions*, 25(3): 1–6. [Online.] Available at: www.highscope.org/file/NewsandInformation/Extensions/ExtVol25No3_low.pdf (accessed: 8 January 2015).

Evans, J. (2013) Using nursery rhymes, jingles, songs and poems as a way into writing. In J. Evans (ed.) *The Writing Classroom: Aspects of Writing and the Primary Child, 3–11*. Abingdon: Routledge, pp. 8–18.

Everson, B.J. (1991) Vygotsky and the teaching of writing. *The Quarterly*, 13(3): 8–11. [Online.] Available at: http://tinyurl.com/onx6av8 (accessed: 15 January 2015).

Fassler, J. (2013) Why Stephen King spends 'months and even years' writing opening sentences. *The Atlantic*, 23 July. [Online.] Available at: www.theatlantic.com/entertainment/archive/2013/07/why-stephen-king-spends-months-and-even-years-writing-opening-sentences/278043/ (accessed: 4 January 2014).

Featherstone, J. (2012) *From Mark Making to Writing*. [Online.] Available at: http://sallyfeatherstone.org/PDFs/Markmakingtowriting.pdf (accessed: 5 April 2015).

Forman, G.E. (2013) Teaching kids about compromise. *VINCIGenius.com*, 21 February. [Online.] Available at: www.vincigenius.com/community/learning-to-compromise/(accessed: 15 January 2015).

Foster, J. (2005) *Word Whirls and Other Shape Poems*. Oxford: Oxford University Press.

Fox, L. and Lentini, R.H. (2006) Teaching children a vocabulary for emotions. *Beyond the Journal*. Young Children on the Web, November. [Online.] Available at: www.naeyc.org/files/yc/file/200611/BTJFoxSupplementalActivities.pdf (accessed: 12 June 2013).

Freedman, C. and Cort, B. (2007) *Aliens Love Underpants*. London: Simon & Schuster UK Ltd.

Freeman, S.W. (2010) 6 ways to hook your readers from the very first line. *Write It Sideways*. [Online.] Available at: http://writeitsideways.com/6-ways-to-hook-your-readers-from-the-very-first-line/ (accessed: 23 January 2015).

Gain, P. (2012) *Stories: Ages 3–5*. Dunstable: Belair Publishing.

Gall, C. (2013) *Awesome Dawson*. New York: Little Brown Books for Young Readers.

Garber, S. (2002) *Memorable Characters…Magnificent Stories*. New York: Scholastic Professional Books.

Garrett, J. (1996) Introduction. In B. Preiss (ed.) *The Best Children's Books in the World: A Treasury of Illustrated Stories*. New York: Abrams, pp. 7–9.

Gervais, R. (2007) *Flaminals*. London: Faber & Faber.

Gilbert, J. (2007) *The Influence of Music on Painting and Animation*. [Online.] Available at: http://ncca.bournemouth.ac.uk/gallery/files/innovations/2007/Gilbert_Jennifer_392/Innovations_JenniferGilbert.pdf (accessed: 1 April 2015).

Gordon, M. (2013) *Little Red Riding Hood*. London: Usborne Publishing.

Goularte, R. (2014) *Lesson Plan: Draw a Story – Stepping from Pictures to Writing*. ReadWriteThink – International Literacy Association/National Council of Teachers of English. [Online.] Available at: www.readwritethink.org/classroom-resources/lesson-plans/draw-story-stepping-from-45.html?tab=1#tabs (accessed: 8 June 2015).

Graham, S. and Perin, D. (2007) *Writing Next: Effective Strategies to Improve Writing of Adolescents in Middle and High Schools – A report to the Carnegie Corporation of New York*. Washington, DC: Alliance for Excellent Education. In General Teaching Council for England (GTC) (2008) *Research for Teachers: Strategies for Improving Pupils' Writing Skills*. [Online.] Available at: http://tinyurl.com/73p4j7r (accessed: 29 December 2014).

Grainger, T. (2005) Teachers as writers: Learning together. *English in Education*, 39(1): 75–87. [Online.] Available at: http://oro.open.ac.uk/16431/2/29CFFB51.pdf (accessed: 30 March 2015).

Graves, A., Semmel, M. and Gerber, M. (1994) The effects of story prompts on the narrative production of students with and without learning disabilities. *Learning Disability Quarterly*, 17(2): 154–164.

Gravett, E. (2007) *Little Mouse's Big Book of Fears*. London: Macmillan Children's Books.

Grossman, J. (2013) What are Snapchat stories? *Information Space*, 10 October. [Online.] Available at: http://infospace.ischool.syr.edu/2013/10/10/what-are-snapchat-stories/ (accessed 23 December 2014).

Hadley-Garcia, G. (2013) 'Extreme' characters fuel the plot of 'The Master'. *The Japan Times*, 5 April. [Online.] Available at: www.japantimes.co.jp/culture/2013/04/05/films/extreme-characters-fuel-the-plot-of-the-master/#.Uba5oL5waM8 (accessed: 11 June 2013).

Haloin, M., Jameson, G., Piccolo, J. and Oosterveen, K. (2005) Genre characteristics. In R. Routman (2005) *Writing Essentials*. Portsmouth, NH: Heinemann. [Online.] Available at: www.ux1.eiu.edu/~cfder/GenreCharacteristicsChart.pdf (accessed: 30 December 2014).

Hamilton, M. and Weiss, M. (2007) *The Stolen Smell*. Atlanta, GA: August House Story Cove.

Hamm, M. (2006) *Winners Never Quit!* London: HarperCollins Children's Books.

Handwriting Without Tears (n.d.) *This is My NAME!* [Online.] Available at: www.hwtears.com/files/Teaching_Children_Their_Name.pdf (accessed: 28 November 2014).

Hardy, J. (2014) An age-old question: How do you show a character's age? *Janice Hardy's Fiction University*, 12 February. [Online.] Available at: http://blog.janicehardy.com/2014/02/an-age-old-question-how-do-you-show.html (accessed: 30 November 2014).

Hargreaves, R. (2008) *Mr. Happy*. London: Egmont.

Harvey, R. (2004) *At the Beach*. Crows Nest, NSW: Allen & Unwin.

Haughton, C. (2013) *A Bit Lost*. London: Walker Books.

Hawkinge Primary School (2013) *Bang!* Amazon CreateSpace Independent Publishing Platform.

Hedderwick, M. (2010) *Katie Morag And The Two Grandmothers*. London: Red Fox.

Helsley, D. (2011) *The Day No One Played Together: A Story About Compromise*. Milwaukee, WI: Mirror Publishing.

Hickman, S. (2014) What is an internal conflict? *eHow*. [Online.] Available at: www.ehow.com/about_5598083_internal-conflict_.html (accessed: 21 April 2014).

Hiles, M., Essex, S., Fox, A. and Luger, C. (2008) The 'words and pictures' storyboard: Making sense for children and families. *Context*, 97: 10–16. [Online.] Available at: http://samenwerkenwijaanveiligheid.nl/wp-content/uploads/2013/05/wordsandpicturesarticle.pdf (accessed: 2 June 2015).

Hill, E. (2009) *Where's Spot?* London: Frederick Warne.

Hill, S. (2006) *Developing Early Literacy: Assessment and Teaching*. Prahran, VIC: Eleanor Curtain Publishing.

Hopwood-Stephens, I. (2013) *Learning on Your Doorstep: Stimulating Writing Through Creative Play Outdoors for Ages 5–9*. Abingdon: Routledge.

Horn, C.V. (n.d.) *Elements of Literature: Point of View*. [Online.] Available at: www.nps.gov/mora/forteachers/upload/background-elements-of-literature_sr.pdf (accessed: 29 December 2014).

Howard, P. and Cigrand, M. (2003) *25 Fun-Filled Collaborative Books Based on Favorite Picture Books: Easy How-To's & Reproducible Patterns for Collaborative Books That Help Kids Respond to Literature – and Build Early Reading & Writing Skills*. New York: Scholastic Professional Books.

Huff, K.J. (2000) *Storytelling with Puppets, Props, and Playful Tales*. Dunstable: Brilliant Publications.

Hughes, J. (2015) *Animal Auditions*. Amazon CreateSpace Independent Publishing Platform.

Humphreys, N. (2013) *Abbie Rose & the Magic Suitcase: The Day a Panda Really Saved My Life*. Singapore: Marshall Cavendish International (Asia) Pte Ltd.

Ings, R. (2009) *Writing is Primary*. [Online.] Available at: http://tinyurl.com/ngjmxty (accessed: 8 April 2015).

Irvine, J. (2005) *Easy-To-Make Pop-Ups*. Mineola, NY: Dover Publications.

Isenberg, J.P. and Jalongo, M.R. (2010) *Types of Children's Conflicts*. [Online.] Available at: www.education.com/reference/article/types-childrens-conflicts/ (accessed: 10 January 2015).

Jasper, M. (2006) *Professional Development, Reflection and Decision-Making*. Oxford: Blackwell Publishing.

Jeffers, O. (2005) *Lost and Found*. London: Philomel Books.

Jindrich, J. (2014) *Story Starters*. [Online.] Available at: www.meddybemps.com/9.700.html (accessed: 25 July 2014).

Johns, L.C. (2004) *The Writing Coach*. Clifton Park, NY: Delmar Learning.

Johnson, J.A. (2014) Important life lessons I have learned from children. *HubPages*. [Online.] Available at: http://julieajohnson.hubpages.com/hub/Important-Lessons-I-have-Learned-From-Children (accessed: 3 August 2014).

Jones, A. (2012) *Action Stories for Children*. [Online.] Available at: www.ihes.com/bcn/tt/eltconf/12/action_stories_with_children.pdf (accessed: 15 January 2015).

Jones, L. (2014) The role weather played on D-Day. *9 WAFB*, 4 July. [Online.] Available at: www.wafb.com/story/25711519/the-role-weather-played-on-d-day (accessed: 31 July 2014).

Jose, P.E. and Brewer, W.F. (1983) *The Development of Story Liking: Character Identification, Suspense and Outcome Resolution*. Technical Report No. 291, University of Illinois. [Online.] Available at: https://www.ideals.illinois.edu/bitstream/handle/2142/17668/ctrstreadtechrepv01983i00291_opt.pdf?sequence=1 (accessed: 26 December 2014).

Juel, C. (1988) Learning to read and write: A longitudinal study of 54 children from first through fourth grades. *Journal of Educational Psychology*, 80(4): 437–447.

Kendell, J. (2004) *SAT Attack Reading/Writing: Teachers Guide*. Oxford: Harcourt Education.

Kerr, J. (2003) *Goodnight Mog*. London: HarperCollins Children's Books.

Kerr, J. (2006) *The Tiger Who Came For Tea*. London: HarperCollins Children's Books.

KidsHealth in the Classroom (2006) *Conflict Resolution*. [Online.] Available at: http://kidshealth.org/classroom/3to5/personal/growing/conflict_resolution.pdf (accessed: 9 January 2015).

Kindergartenteacherclaire (2010) Sentence starters. *Thoughts from a Kindergarten Teacher – Now a First Grade Teacher*, 28 January. [Online.] Available at: http://kindergartenteacherclaire.wordpress.com/2010/01/28/sentence-starters/ (accessed: 23 March 2014).

Kipling, R. and Davis, L. (1992) *Rikki-Tikki-Tavi*. San Diego, CA: Harcourt Children's Books.

Klems, B. (2012) The 7 rules of picking names for fictional characters. *Writer's Digest*, 28 August. [Online.] Available at: www.writersdigest.com/online-editor/the-7-rules-of-picking-names-for-fictional-characters (accessed: 24 March 2015).

Knapton, S. (2014) Reading fairy stories to children is harmful, says Richard Dawkins. *The Telegraph*, 4 June. [Online.] Available at: www.telegraph.co.uk/news/science/science-news/10875912/Reading-fairy-stories-to-children-is-harmful-says-Richard-Dawkins.html (accessed: 7 January 2015).

Krebs, L. (2011) *We're Roaming in the Rainforest*. Oxford: Barefoot Books Ltd.

Kreidler, W.J. and Whittall, S.T. (1999) *Adventures in Peacemaking. A Conflict Resolution Activity Guide for Early Childhood Educators*, 2nd edition. Cambridge, MA: Educators for Social Responsibility.

Laniyan-Amoako, O. (2010) Black publisher fights to bring more books to black and ethnic minority readers. *Caribbean Book Blog*, 6 March. [Online.] Available at: https://caribbeanbookblog.wordpress.com/2010/03/06/black-publisher-fights-to-bring-more-books-to-black-and-ethnic-minority-readers/ (accessed: 30 November 2014).

LearningExpress (2003) *501 Writing Prompts*. [Online.] Available at: www.misd.net/languageart/grammarinaction/501writingprompts.pdf (accessed: 20 January 2015).

Lehrhaupt, A. (2013) *Warning: Do Not Open This Book!* New York: Simon & Schuster Books for Young Readers.

Leonard, E. (2010) *10 Rules of Writing*. London: Weidenfeld & Nicolson.

Lester, H. (1992) *Me First!* New York: Houghton Mifflin Company.

LifeCare (2011) *Conflict Resolution*. [Online.] Available at: www.wfm.noaa.gov/workplace/EmotionalIntell_Handout_4.pdf (accessed: 24 January 2015).

London, J. (2013) *Love of Life*. Amazon CreateSpace Independent Publishing Platform.

Lopez, L. (n.d.) Fantastical Beasts. *The J. Paul Getty Museum*. [Online.] Available at: www.getty.edu/education/teachers/classroom_resources/curricula/arts_lang_arts/a_la_lesson35.html (accessed: 26 May 2014).

Lopresti, A. (2008) *Fantastical Creatures Field Guide: How to Hunt Them Down and Draw Them Where They Live*. New York: Watson-Guptill.

Lucke, M. (1999) *Schaum's Quick Guide to Writing Great Short Stories*. New York: McGraw Hill. [Online.] Available at: http://tinyurl.com/n34ps8f (accessed: 8 September 2014).

Malindine, D. (2012) *Tutor Master Helps You Write Stories: Book One*. Middlesex: Tutor Master Services.

Marron, J.E. (2010) *Using Wordless Books to Help Emergent Literacy Skills*. [Online.] Available at: http://fisherpub.sjfc.edu/cgi/viewcontent.cgi?article=1008&context=education_ETD_masters (accessed: 25 July 2014).

Martin, B., Jnr (1997) *Brown Bear, Brown Bear, What Do You See?* London: Puffin.

Martin, L.J. (2011) Themes in children's fiction. *Literature For Kids*. [Online.] Available at: www.literature4kids.com/themes-in-childrens-fiction (accessed: 14 December 2014).

Mathieson, K. (2005) *Social Skills in the Early Years: Supporting Social and Behavioural Learning*. London: Sage.

Matthews, A. (2003) *A Midsummer Night's Dream: A Shakespeare Story*. London: Orchard Books.

Mayer, M. (2014) *We All Need Forgiveness*. Nashville, TN: Tommy Nelson.

Mayesky, M. (2014) *Creative Activities and Curriculum for Young Children*, 11th edition. Boston, MA: Cengage Learning.

Maynard, T. (2002) *Boys and Literacy: Exploring the Issues*. London: RoutledgeFalmer.

Maynes, N. and Julien-Schultz, L. (2011) The impact of visual frameworks on teacher candidates' professional reflection. *LEARNing Landscapes*, 5(1): 193–210.

McBratney, S. (2001) *I'm Sorry*. London: HarperCollins Children's Books.

McCarthy, T. (1998) *Narrative Writing*. New York: Scholastic.

McKee, D. (2007) *Elmer*. London: Anderson Press Ltd.

McKee, D. (2012) *Not Now, Bernard!* London: Anderson Press.

Meiners, C.J. (2003) *Share and Take Turns*. Minneapolis, MN: Free Spirit Publishing Inc.

Miller, S. and Pennycuff, L. (2008) The power of story: Using storytelling to improve literacy learning. *Journal of Cross-Disciplinary Perspectives in Education*, 1(1): 36–43. [Online.] Available at: http://jcpe.wmwikis.net/file/view/miller.pdf (accessed: 7 April 2015).

Mills, J.C. (2003) *Gentle Willow: A Story for Children About Dying*, 2nd edition. Washington, DC: Magination Press.

Misra, A. and R, N. (2012) Conflicts with the supernatural. *The Hindu*, 26 June. [Online.] Available at: http://tinyurl.com/opyc85r (accessed: 7 January 2015).

Moore, J. (2005) *Teaching Sentence Structure to Primary Writers*. [Online.] Available at: www.scribd.com/doc/69665814/Teaching-Sentence-Structure-Part-One#scribd (accessed: 2 June 2015).

Morris, R. (1993) Sentence strips. *Writing Notebook: Visions for Learning*, 11(1): 35–38.

Morris, R. (2013) Music tells me stories – the undercover soundtrack. *Writers & Artists: The Insider Guide to the Media*, 16 July. [Online.] Available at: https://www.writersandartists.co.uk/2013/07/music-tells-me-stories-the-undercover-soundtrack-by-roz-morris (accessed: 5 April 2014).

Murphy, J. (2007) *Peace at Last*. London: Macmillan Children's Books.

National Literacy Trust (n.d.a) *Story Boxes*. [Online.] Available at: www.literacytrust.org.uk/assets/0000/3211/Story_box_guide.pdf (accessed: 3 May 2014).

National Literacy Trust (n.d.b) *Story Sacks*. [Online.] Available at: www.literacytrust.org.uk/assets/0000/3210/Story_sack_guide.pdf (accessed: 7 September 2014).

Newcombe, R. (2013) Learning about vehicles and transport. *Early Childhood Education*, 7 August. [Online.] Available at: www.earlychildhoodeducation.co.uk/learning-about-vehicles-transport.html (accessed: 3 May 2014).

North, K. (2015) May I have a compromise? *Empowered to Connect*. [Online.] Available at: http://empoweredtoconnect.org/may-i-have-a-compromise/(accessed: 15 January 2015).

NSW Health (2009) *The Physical Activity Handbook: Preschoolers*. [Online.] Available at: www.imagineeducation.com.au/files/GapTraining/Good_20for_20Kids__20Physical_20Activity_20Handbook.pdf (accessed: 15 January 2015).

OECD (2013) *Country Note: United Kingdom – Results from PISA 2012*. [Online.] Available at: www.oecd.org/unitedkingdom/PISA-2012-results-UK.pdf (accessed: 5 April 2015).

OFSTED (2009) *English at the Crossroads: An Evaluation of English in Primary and Secondary Schools, 2005/08*. [Online.] Available at: http://dera.ioe.ac.uk/298/1/English%20at%20the%20crossroads.pdf (accessed: 5 April 2015).

OFSTED (2014) *The Report of Her Majesty's Chief Inspector of Education, Children's Services and Skills 2013/14: Schools*. [Online.] Available at: www.gov.uk/government/uploads/system/uploads/attachment_data/file/384707/Ofsted_Annual_Report_201314_Schools.pdf (accessed: 3 April 2015)

Oh My Disney (2013) *What We Learned From Toy Story*. 23 March. [Online.] Available at: http://tinyurl.com/osw3apg (accessed: 3 August 2014).

Paradise, J.L. (2007) *An analysis of improving student performance through the use of registered therapy dogs serving as motivators for reluctant readers*. Doctoral dissertation. [Online.] Available at: http://etd.fcla.edu/CF/CFE0001561/Paradise_Julie_L_200705_Ed.D.pdf (accessed: 31 March 2015).

Parkes, B. (2001) *Who's in the Shed?* Maidenhead: Kingscourt/McGraw-Hill.

Parlakian, R. and Lerner, C. (2010) Beyond Twinkle, Twinkle: Using music with infants and toddlers. *Young Children*, March, 14–19. [Online.] Available at: www.naeyc.org/content/music (accessed: 21 January 2015).

Paton, G. (2012) Parents 'shun bedtime reading' in favour of TV. *The Telegraph*, 19 October. [Online.] Available at: www.telegraph.co.uk/education/educationnews/9617868/Parents-shun-bedtime-reading-in-favour-of-TV.html (accessed: 2 April 2015).

Patterson, R. (2012) *My Big Shouting Day*. London: Jonathan Cape.

Peat, A. (2002) *Improving Story Writing at Key Stages 1 & 2*. Oxford: Nash Pollock Publishing.

Peat, A. (2010) *Beyond 'Happily Ever After': Improving the Ending of Narrative Texts*. [Online.] Available at: www.alanpeat.com/resources/ending.html (accessed: 6 December 2014).

Peha, S. (2003a) *The Five Facts of Fiction*. [Online.] Available at: www.ttms.org/PDFs/10%20Five%20Facts%20of%20Fiction%20v001%20(Full).pdf (accessed: 29 December 2014).

Peha, S. (2003b) *The Writing Teacher's Strategy Guide*. [Online.] Available at: www.ttms.org/PDFs/01%20Writing%20Strategy%20Guide%20v001%20(Full).pdf (accessed: 6 December 2014).

Pett, M. and Rubinstein, G. (2012) *The Girl Who Never Made Mistakes*. Naperville, IL: Sourcebooks, Jaberwocky.

Pienkowski, J. (1981) *Robot*. London: Heinemann Young Books.

Polka Theatre (n.d.) *The Jolly Postman: Activity Pack*. [Online.] Available at: http://tinyurl.com/mrc3dpg (accessed: 25 February 2015).

Pullman, P. (2012) *Grimm Tales: For Young and Old*. London: Penguin Books.

Ribena Plus (2012) The role of toys in play (Chapter 3). In *The Ribena Plus Play Report*. [Online.] Available at: www.ribena.co.uk/download/Ribena_Plus_Play_Report_Ch3.pdf (accessed: 23 June 2013).

Richardson, J. (1995) Avoidance as an active mode of conflict resolution. *Team Performance Management: An International Journal*, 1(4): 19–25.

Rickerty, S. (2014) *Crayon*. London: Simon & Schuster.

Rinzler, A. (2011) Grand finales: Tips for writing great endings. *The Book Deal*, 31 December. [Online.] Available at: www.alanrinzler.com/blog/2011/12/31/grand-finales-tips-for-writing-great-endings/(accessed: 3 January 2015).

Roberts, A. (2012) *The Little Book of Props for Writing*. London: A&C Black.

Robinson, H. (2005) *Mixed Up Fairy Tales*. London: Hodder Children's Books.

Rockliff, M. (2014) *The Grudge Keeper*. Atlanta, GA: Peachtree Publishers.

Roddy, L. (2003) *How to Write a Story: A Step-by-Step Method for Understanding and Teaching Basic Story Writing Techniques*. Atascadero, CA: Institute for Excellence in Writing, Inc. [Online.] Available at: www.writing-edu.com/writing/PDF%20samples/HWS_sample.pdf (accessed: 5 December 2014).

Rosen, M. (1997) *We're Going on a Bear Hunt*. London: Walker Books.

Rosen, M. (2004) *Michael Rosen's Sad Book*. London: Walker Books.

Ross, A. (2010) *Nutrition and Its Effects on Academic Performance: How Can Our Schools Improve?* [Online.] Available at: www.nmu.edu/sites/DrupalEducation/files/UserFiles/Files/Pre-Drupal/SiteSections/Students/GradPapers/Projects/Ross_Amy_MP.pdf (accessed: 25 February 2015).

Ross, T. (2012) *I Want to Win!* London: Anderson Press.

Rowling, J.K. (2001) *Fantastic Beasts and Where to Find Them*. London: Bloomsbury Publishing.

Rubin, J. (2012) *Conflicts With Ourselves: Lessons From Charlie Brown*. 8 December. [Online.] Available at: http://drjeffreyrubin.wordpress.com/2012/12/08/conflicts-with-ourselves-lessons-from-charlie-brown/ (accessed: 21 April 2014).

Rumseya, I. and Ballarda, K.D. (1985) Teaching self-management strategies for independent story writing to children with classroom behaviour difficulties. *Educational Psychology: An International Journal of Experimental Educational Psychology*, 5(2): 147–157.

Rylands, T. (2008) Colourful stories. *Times Educational Supplement*, 12 May. [Online.] Available at: www.tes.co.uk/article.aspx?storycode=2177846 (accessed: 31 March 2015).

Saltzberg, B. (2008) *Crazy Hair Day*. Somerville, MA: Candlewick Press.

Sambuchino, C. (2013) The worst ways to begin your novel: Advice from literary agents. *TheWriteLife*, 6 August. [Online.] Available at: http://thewritelife.com/the-worst-ways-to-begin-your-novel-advice-from-literary-agents/#RQjp2k:pqL (accessed: 3 January 2015).

Santoso, A. (2009) 7 brilliant ideas scribbled on cocktail napkins and toilet papers. *Neatorama*, 5 March. [Online.] Available at: www.neatorama.com/2009/03/05/7-brilliant-ideas-scribbled-on-cocktail-napkins-and-toilet-papers/ (accessed: 30 November 2014).

Saunders, M., Lewis, P. and Thornhill A. (2009) *Research Methods for Business Students*, 5th edition. Harlow: Pearson Education.

Schneider, J.J. and Jackson, S.A.W. (2000) Process drama: A special space and place for writing. *The Reading Teacher*, 54(1): 38–51.

Seeger, L.V. (2015) *Bully*. London: Anderson Press.

Selznick, R. (2012) *School Struggles: A Guide to Your Shut-Down Learner's Success*. Boulder, CO: Sentiant Publications.

Seuss, Dr. (2001) *My Many Coloured Days*. London: Red Fox.

Shah, A. and Godiyal, S. (n.d.) *ICT in the Early Years: Balancing the risks and benefits*. [Online.] Available at: www.aiaer.net/ejournal/vol21209/17.%20Shah%20&%20Godiyal.pdf (accessed: 11 June 2015).

Shaw, R. (2007) *How to Write Wonderful Stories (Junior Primary)*. Hillarys, W. Australia: Intelligent Australia Productions. [Online.] Available at: https://australianteacher.files.wordpress.com/2011/01/how-to-write-wonderful-stories-junior-primary.pdf (accessed: 5 April 2015).

Shaw, R. (2008) *1001 Brilliant Writing Ideas: Teaching Inspirational Story-Writing for All Ages*. Abingdon: Routledge.

Shipton, J. (1999) *What If?* London: Macmillan Children's Books.

Shoshan, B. (2004) *Memory Bottles*. London: Meadowside Children's Books.

Sidman, J. (2011) *Swirl by Swirl: Spirals in Nature*. New York: Houghton Mifflin Harcourt.

Sierra, J. (2000) *The Beautiful Butterfly*. New York: Clarion Books.

Silvey, A. (ed.) (1995) *Children's Books and Their Creators*. New York: Houghton Mifflin Company.

Singleton, R.S. and Conrad, J.A. (2000) *Filmmaker's Dictionary*, 2nd edition. Ed. J.W. Healy. Hollywood, CA: Lone Eagle Publishing Company.

Sipe, L.R. (1993) Using transformations of traditional stories: Making the reading–writing connection. *The Reading Teacher*, 47(1): 18–26. [Online.] Available at: http://tinyurl.com/m8m4ok2 (accessed: 22 January 2015).

Slegers, L. (2012) *Kevin's Big Book of the Five Senses*. New York: Clavis Publishing Inc.

Smith, F. (1982) *Writing and the Writer*. New York: Holt, Rinehart and Winston.

Smith, M., Segal, R. and Segal, J. (2014) Phobias and fears: Symptoms, treatment, and self-help for phobias and fears. *Helpguide.org*, December. [Online.] Available at: www.helpguide.org/articles/anxiety/phobias-and-fears.htm (accessed: 5 December 2014).

Snicket, L. (2006) *A Series of Unfortunate Events*. London: Egmont.

Soar Higher (2006) *SOAR Stories*. [Online.] Available at: www.soarhigheraspen.com/docs/SOAR_Stories.pdf (accessed: 5 December 2014).

Stevens, J. (2012) *Storytelling and Storymaking*. London: Practical Pre-School Books.

Stewart, D.J. (2013) Drawing and story telling with a purple crayon. *Teach Preschool*, 9 September. [Online.] Available at: www.teachpreschool.org/2013/09/drawing-and-story-telling-with-a-purple-crayon/ (accessed: 8 December 2014).

Strauss, L.L. (2010) *Drop Everything and Write! An Easy Breezy Guide for Kids Who Want to Write a Story*. Sausalito, CA: E & E Publishing.

Sturrock, D. (2010) *Storyteller: The Life of Roald Dahl*. London: HarperPress.

Tamburrini, J., Willig, J. and Butler, C. (1984) Children's conceptions of writing. In H. Cowie (ed.) *The Development of Children's Creative Writing*. London: Croom Helm, pp. 188–199.

Taylor, M.A. (2010) *The Monster Chronicles: The role of children's stories featuring monsters in managing childhood fears and promoting empowerment*. Dissertation, Queensland University of Technology. [Online.] Available at: http://eprints.qut.edu.au/37305/1/Michelle_Taylor_Thesis.pdf (accessed: 7 January 2015).

Teacher Support Force (2011) Strategies for teaching writing should include school wide events. *Teacher Support Force*. [Online.] Available at: www.teacher-support-force.com/strategies-for-teaching-writing.html (accessed: 16 October 2014).

TeachUSWrite (2008) Teaching kids to write fantastic hooks. *A to Z Teacher Stuff*, 18 February. [Online.] Available at: http://forums.atozteacherstuff.com/showthread.php?t=53699 (accessed: 3 June 2015).

Temean, K. (2010) Adding an ethnic character to your story. *Writing and Illustrating*, 25 October. [Online.] Available at: http://kathytemean.wordpress.com/2010/10/25/adding-an-ethnic-minority-character-to-your-story/ (accessed: 30 November 2014).

The J. Paul Getty Trust (n.d.) Telling stories in art. *The J. Paul Getty Museum*. [Online.] Available at: www.getty.edu/education/teachers/classroom_resources/curricula/stories/index.html (accessed: 8 December 2014).

The Open University (2014) Writing what you know. *OpenLearn*. [Online.] Available at: www.open.edu/openlearn/history-the-arts/culture/literature-and-creative-writing/creative-writing/writing-what-you-know/content-section-3.1 (accessed: 23 December 2014).

Thomas, P. (2010) *I Can Do It!* London: Wayland.

Thompson, L. (2012) *The Forgiveness Garden*. New York: Feiwel & Friends.

Thornberg, R. (2006) The Situated Nature of Preschool Children's Conflict Strategies. *Educational Psychology*, 26(1): 109–126. [Online.] Available at: www.diva-portal.org/smash/get/diva2:18193/FULLTEXT01.pdf (accessed: 9 January 2015).

Tower Hamlets EMA Team in collaboration with Tower Hamlets teachers (2009) *Progression in Language Structures*. [Online.] Available via: www.communicationacrosscultures.com/82-home/160-progression-in-language-structures (accessed: 3 April 2015).

TRUCE (2009–2010) *Toys, Play & Young Children: Action Guide*. [Online.] Available at: www.truceteachers.org/toyguides/T_Guide_web_09.pdf (accessed: 27 September 2013).

Vandergrift, K.E. (1997) *Children Writing & Publishing*. 15 April. [Online.] Available at: http://comminfo.rutgers.edu/professional-development/childlit/childpublishing.html (accessed: 27 April 2014).

Vertsman, M. (2014) Around the World in 80+ Children's Books. *New York Public Library*, 22 July. [Online.] Available at: www.nypl.org/blog/2014/07/22/around-world-childrens-books (accessed: 11 January 2014).

VIA University College (2013) *Animation as a Learning Tool*. [Online.] Available at: www.viauc.com/schools-faculties/faculty-of-education-and-social-studies/exchange-programmes/Pages/animation-as-a-learning-tool.aspx (accessed: 16 January 2015).

Village Hat Shop (2015) *Hats and children's literature*. [Online.] Available at: www.villagehatshop.com/content/332/hats-and-childrens-literature.html (accessed: 12 June 2015).

Ward, V. (2013) Black characters put parents off books, new Children's Laureate says. *The Telegraph*, 4 June. [Online.] Available at: www.telegraph.co.uk/culture/books/10098595/

Black-characters-put-parents-off-books-new-Childrens-Laureate-says.html   (accessed: 30 November 2014).

Wenner, M. (2009) The serious need for play. *Scientific American Mind.* February. [Online.] Available at: www.scientificamerican.com/article.cfm?id=the-serious-need-for-play (accessed: 26 September 2013).

Whitaker, C. (n.d.) *Best Practices in Teaching Writing.* [Online.] Available at: www.learner. org/workshops/middlewriting/images/pdf/HomeBestPrac.pdf (accessed: 14 October 2014).

Whitin, D.J. and Whitin, P. (2004) *New Visions for Linking Literature and Mathematics.* Reston, VA: National Council of Teachers of Mathematics.

Whybrow, I. (2008) *Along Came a Bedtime.* London: Orchard Books.

Whybrow, I. (2009) *Say Hello to the Dinosaurs!* London: Macmillan Children's Books.

Wilhelm, J.D. (2013) *Improving Comprehension with Think-Aloud Strategies: Modeling What Good Readers Do.* New York: Scholastic.

Williams, L. (1986) *The Little Old Lady Who Was Not Afraid of Anything.* New York: HarperTrophy.

Wilson, G. (2013) *Breaking Through Barriers to Boys' Achievement*, 2nd edition. London: Bloomsbury Education.

Wilson, R.E., Jnr (2012) Play the 'What If?' Game. *Psychology Today*, 10 September. [Online.] Available at: www.psychologytoday.com/blog/the-main-ingredient/201209/play-the-what-if-game (accessed: 22 December 2014).

Wiltshire Council (n.d.) *Support for Writing: Strands 9 to 11 – Years 1 to 6.* [Online.] Available at: www.wiltshire.gov.uk/support-for-writing.pdf (accessed: 5 April 2015).

Winter, J.K. and Winter, E.J. (2009) *A Study of the Effect of Paper Color on Test Performance in Business Communication.* [Online.] Available at: http://rwahlers.iweb.bsu.edu/abd2009/Papers/p09_winter_winter.pdf (accessed: 19 May 2014).

Wiseman, R. (2014) *Night School.* London: Macmillan.

Woledge, S. (2013) A Harrods hamper, Tiffany necklace and a spa day: What competitive parents are buying for their children's teachers as end of year gifts. *Daily Mail*, 17 July. [Online.] Available at: http://tinyurl.com/qan5mos (accessed: 10 August 2014).

Wright, A. (1997) *Creating Stories with Children.* Oxford: Oxford University Press.

Zike, D. (2008) *Dinah Zike's Foldables.* New York: Macmillan/McGraw-Hill.

Index